MARLBOROUGH

JOHN CHURCHILL, 1st DUKE OF MARLBOROUGH

*(From the marble bust by Rysbrack in the National
Portrait Gallery)*

MARLBOROUGH

BY

THE HON. SIR JOHN FORTESCUE

LL.D., D.Litt.

WITH A FRONTISPIECE AND SEVEN MAPS

The Naval & Military Press Ltd

in association with

The National Army Museum, London

Published jointly by

The Naval & Military Press Ltd
Unit 10 Ridgewood Industrial Park,
Uckfield, East Sussex,
TN22 5QE England

Tel: +44 (0) 1825 749494
Fax: +44 (0) 1825 765701

www.naval-military-press.com
www.military-genealogy.com
www.militarymaproom.com

and

The National Army Museum, London
www.national-army-museum.ac.uk

I

THERE is a kind of convention that an eminent Englishman should be able to trace his lineage to ancestors who came over with the Conqueror ; and the foremost biographer of John Churchill has endeavoured to do as much for him with indifferent success. Howbeit it is certain that the Churchills were established in Devon in the fourteenth century, and that from thence one branch of them spread to Dorset. They were, in fact, little country squires ; and it is chiefly the sons of little country squires who have made England great and have built up the British Empire.

John Churchill, grandfather, and Winston Churchill, father of the future Duke of Marlborough, both embraced the King's side in the Civil War, and suffered heavily in pocket from it. Heavy fines, however, did not deter Winston from marrying, during the continuance of internal troubles, the daughter of Sir John Drake of Ashe in Devon ; and at Ashe was born his eldest child, Arabella, in February 1648. A little son, who died in infancy, followed Arabella in 1649 ; and on the 24th of June 1650—just two days before Oliver Cromwell was appointed Captain-General for the Scottish campaign— another little son came into the world, who was baptized at Ashe by the name of John.

We know nothing of his childhood, and can only imagine a beautiful fair-haired boy looking with great grey eyes upon rather dismal sur-roundings. He was educated by his father, who dabbled in literature, and by the parish parson, who taught him his catechism and ex-pounded to him the errors of Rome ; and he learned at least to write a great sprawling hand which retained something of the schoolboy to the end. After ten years the means of the family improved. The Restoration came ; Winston recovered some of his confiscated pro-perty, and after a time obtained a subordinate post at the Court of Charles II. He was able thus to secure for his daughter Arabella the place of maid of honour to the Duchess of York, and for his son John that of page to the Duke.

John Churchill early manifested a passion for soldiering ; and, through the favour of his master, he obtained a commission as ensign in the regiment now called the Grenadier Guards on 14th September 1667. He sought active

6

employment by volunteering for service at Tangier, where the garrison was constantly engaged in petty combats, by no means always successful, with the Moors, and so gained first experience of warfare. But he appears not to have stayed there very long, and returned to his old place about the Duke of York until 1672, when France and England declared war upon Holland. A force of six thousand men under the Duke of Monmouth was sent across the North Sea to join the French Army, Churchill accompanying it as a Captain in the High Admiral's, that is to say, James's own regiment. Though the French were led by three such great commanders as Condé, Turenne and Luxemburg, the operations were feeble, being dictated by Louis xiv. himself, while the Dutch resistance was of the feeblest. Churchill is said to have been prominent for brave conduct in a small affair at the siege of Nimeguen in 1672, and he certainly spent the winter of 1672-3 in Paris. He had by that time been transferred to an English regiment in the French service, with which he again distinguished himself at the siege of Maastricht in June 1673. In 1674 he was promoted Colonel of this regiment, and he seems to have served with it under Turenne in Germany, and after Turenne's death in

7

1675 under other commanders. But little is
known about this part of his career. It appears
that he was frequently in England, and that
he was promoted both in the Duke of York's
household and in his regiment, for he became
Lieutenant-colonel in January 1675. It is
only certain that he was a Colonel of infantry
in the French service, that he had at least some
opportunity of studying the methods of the
greatest of living captains, and that he learned
to speak and write bad French with fluency
and confidence.

In 1678 Charles II. decided to send troops
to aid the Dutch against the French, and
Churchill, promoted full Colonel on 17th February, was appointed to command a portion of
them. But this was the least important event of
this year of his life. The most important was his
marriage to Sarah Jennings, the less beautiful
of two beautiful sisters who had both of them
been taken into the household of the Duchess
of York. Sarah had been but twelve years of
age when she first began life at Court, and had
been made companion to Princess Anne ; she
was only fifteen when Churchill, ten years her
senior, fell desperately in love with her and
she with him. But there were difficulties about
money and difficulties about consent of parents ;

and not until early in 1678 did the pair con-
trive to get married, even then secretly, though
in presence of the Duchess of York. The
second incident of moment in this year was
that Churchill was despatched on a secret
mission to the Prince of Orange, whereby two
of the ablest men in Europe were able to take
the measure of each other. They were of the
same age. One of them had been called upon
at the age of twenty-one to take command of
the United Provinces at a moment of supreme
peril, and had compassed their salvation by
sheer courage and force of will. But William
of Orange had been born to great place. He
was not only Stadtholder of his own provinces,
with very wide powers, but he was nephew of
the King of England. In 1673 he had married
an English princess, Mary, daughter of the
Duke of York ; and already there were many
in England who hoped to see him on the English
throne.

The other, John Churchill, being but the
son of an impoverished country squire, had to
make his way for himself. He had vast ambition and great natural advantages. The pretty
boy had become an extraordinarily handsome
man, with the long curled locks of the time
framing a complexion as fresh as a girl's, fine

9

grey eyes, a noble brow, and a very well formed mouth and chin. His good looks alone would have sufficed to turn the head of any woman ; and to these he added irresistible personal charm. He was invincibly sweet-tempered, patient and gentle, hated quarrels and ab-horred discourtesy ; and behind these outward qualities, which of themselves count for so much, there was a resolute will and transcen-dent common sense. Yet his position was difficult and the outlook was uncertain. He owed his start in life to his patron the Duke of York ; he was bound to him by many ties, and in considerable measure depended upon him for advancement. But James was the most unpopular man in England. It cannot have been pleasant to serve James. I have never seen a portrait of him from childhood upwards —and he was a beautiful child—which does not wear a peevish expression. There may have been some physical cause at the back of this, but the fact remains. He had his redeem-ing qualities. He was a keen sportsman, and he proved himself a good soldier, a good sailor, and a really able departmental administrator. But he had a nasty temper and was perverse and wrong-headed. Moreover, he was of course a bigoted Catholic at a time when the tyranny of Catholicism was still dreaded, and when Englishmen held that nothing really was of supreme importance except religious opinions. Before Churchill had been married much more than a year the Commons brought in a bill to exclude James from the succession to the throne ; but even before that, James had been obliged to withdraw first to the Netherlands and then to Scotland. Churchill, who accompanied him, was charged with many important missions to the King on behalf of his brother, until in 1682 James, having apparently triumphed over his enemies, was able to return to the Court in London. In reward for his services, Churchill was created Lord Churchill of Eyemouth, in Scotland, and on the 19th November 1683 was appointed to be Colonel of the Royal Dragoons, which had just been called into existence.

This gave him an addition to his income, for a colonel in those days, and indeed even one hundred and sixty years later, was entitled to make a profit, if he could, out of the annual clothing of his regiment. Money must have been a constant anxiety to him. He was still dependent almost entirely upon his salaries as a member of James's household and as Colonel of a regiment ; and, though the payment of the latter was fairly certain, salaries in general were in those times and for a full century later most irregularly paid. No comfortable cheque arrived at the end of every month or quarter, but, upon petition, an order of some kind was issued, often very late, upon some office or other ; and the holder of that order was fortunate if, after long delay, he received his cash, very fortunate indeed if he received it in full. Moreover, Churchill might forfeit all his emoluments if he chanced to give offence to the King or to the Duke of York. Finally, his wife had by this time presented him with two little girls, so that he had given additional hostages to fortune ; and the future was uncertain as ever.

II

CHARLES II. died in 1685, and upon the corona-
tion of James, Churchill received an English
peerage with the title of Lord Churchill of Sand-
ridge. Then came the rebellion of Monmouth,
which was, practically, put down by Churchill,
who made good the mistakes of his superior at
Sedgemoor. In July 1685 he was promoted
Major-General, a mere accession of rank which
gave him no increase of pay. Then James
entered upon his fatal policy of favouring
popery and introducing autocratic government, in which he persisted, despite of
Churchill's warnings. At the end of June 1688
a number of leading statesmen sent an invita-
tion to William of Orange to come over with an
army and defend the liberties of England, and
on the 4th of August Churchill likewise wrote
to him to throw in his own lot upon William's
side. He exerted himself to carry with him
some of the principal officers of the Army, but
remained with James until after the landing
of William, when he deserted to the Prince of

Orange's quarters. Through his persuasion likewise, Princess Anne, with Lady Churchill in attendance, forsook her father and took refuge with her brother-in-law and cousin. A fortnight later, on the 11th of December, James fled from England and the Revolution was accomplished.

Beyond question this is an unpleasant passage in Marlborough's life. It was not only that he deserted James—he frankly used the word in the letter which he wrote to the King upon his departure—but that he remained with him, dissimulating his disloyalty, for more than three months after he made up his mind to do so, and contrived that the blow, when it did fall, should be decisive. That he or any other one man could have saved James is not, I think, to be thought of. That Churchill took the patriotic course is unquestionable, for a very short continuance of James's reign would have led to civil war. After all, James was displaced only to make room for his daughters ; and it was reasonable to expect that one or the other of these would produce an heir. Beyond all doubt, too, Churchill felt strongly about the maintenance of the Protestant religion in England, and was no friend to arbitrary government. But that the furtherance of his own

14

career had no part in his determination, it would be absurd to suppose. He meant to rise high, for he could not have been unconscious of his own powers ; and he saw his best chance in attaching himself to the side which he thought most likely to win. It was his misfortune that he began life penniless, and found himself from boyhood in a position of dependence. Perhaps only those who have started under the same disadvantages have any right to judge him.

Churchill was rewarded by William with a small appointment at Court, and on the 9th of April 1689 with the Earldom of Marlborough, by which name he shall be called in future. Meanwhile, upon hearing of William's invasion of England, France had declared war against the United Provinces ; and, though most of the British Army was required in Ireland, it was decided to send ten battalions to join the Dutch and their Allies in Holland under command of Marlborough. The troops started in April, and Marlborough followed them at the end of May. The British Army generally was at this time in a shocking state, and the detachment in the Low Countries was no exception to the rule. But under Marlborough it improved ; and the French commander,

Marshal d'Humières, attempting to surprise the post of Walcourt, which was under Marlborough's charge, found himself outmanœuvred and repelled with considerable loss. This, Marlborough's first brush with a Marshal of France, won him high praise both from the Commander-in-Chief on the spot and from William.

In 1690 he was appointed Lieutenant-General of all the forces in England during the King's absence in Ireland, and going himself to Ireland in the autumn, by sheer skill besieged and captured Cork and Kinsale within six weeks. In the course of these operations he took note of a young officer named William Cadogan. In 1691 he accompanied William to a futile campaign in Flanders, holding command of the British contingent ; but even so, his military ability profoundly impressed the veteran generals of the Continent among whom he was thrown. Nevertheless, before the close of the operations he was superseded ; and early in the next year he fell into complete disgrace, being dismissed from all his appointments civil and military. In May he was even confined in the Tower for a few weeks, and upon his liberation found himself still banished from the Court. There was good cause for this. Marlborough, in common with several leaders of the Revolution, had sought and to all appearance achieved reconciliation with the exiled James. William had disappointed them. He cared nothing for England except as an important piece in the game against France, and had done more for his Dutch favourites than for his English supporters, for whom, with the exception of Marlborough, he felt a deep and excusable contempt. But Marlborough he feared as a man great enough to be a possible rival. It is most unlikely that Marlborough designed to recall James to the throne, but it is possible that he hoped to oust William and replace him by Anne, who would be a pliant instrument in his hands—to anticipate, in fact, the state of things which was actually brought about by William's death. In any case, William decided to have nothing more to do with Marlborough for the present ; and Marlborough on his side continued to keep in touch with James. No one can blame William, though it was a misfortune for England, and perhaps for Europe, that he did not send Marlborough to command the Allied troops in the Low Countries instead of commanding them in person with very indifferent success. But the English did not love the Dutch, and a victorious Marlborough returning from a brilliant campaign with every English soldier at his feet would have been a very dangerous competitor.

So Marlborough remained in the background, a poor as well as a disgraced man, until 1697, when with some reluctance William approved of his appointment to be Governor to William, Duke of Gloucester, the only one of Anne's many children who lived into a sickly and shortly-ended boyhood. Marlborough's biographer states that his military rank and employments were restored to him ; but he received no regiment in lieu of that which had been taken from him, and a General Officer in those days received no pay as such. He was, however, reinstated in the privy council, and he was further nominated one of the lords justices to execute the sovereign's functions during William's absence abroad. Altogether, William had evidently decided to trust him, knowing that, in the situation of European affairs, he could not do without him.

The war ceased temporarily by the signature of the Peace of Ryswick in 1697. William was thereby acknowledged by France as King of England, and Anne as his successor ; and practically that was all. It was not a peace but a truce, the result of exhaustion, and both

Louis xiv. and William frankly recognised the fact. Louis was still bent upon making France mistress of Europe, and William was still as resolute to thwart him ; and there was a ground of quarrel which might in the near future set them again at each other's throats. King Charles ii. of Spain was nearing his end, and there were three claimants to succession to his crown : the Emperor Leopold i., the Electoral Prince of Bavaria, and the Dauphin, each of them descended from a Spanish princess. The peace of Europe demanded an equitable division of the Spanish possessions between them ; and in 1698, after much negotiation, France, Holland and England agreed upon such a division. The arrangement was presently cancelled by the death of the Electoral Prince, and the negotiators, meeting again, agreed in 1700 to a second partition. But in this year 1700, momentous events followed quickly one upon another. In October the little Duke of Gloucester died, leaving the Protestant succession uncertain ; and in November the King of Spain likewise died, bequeathing his empire to Philip, grandson of Louis xiv., upon the sole condition that he should renounce the throne of France for himself and his heirs. Louis after some hesitation accepted the bequest,

19

while rejecting the condition ; and therewith it seemed likely that France would become mistress not of Europe only but of the world. The possession of Spain alone sufficed to exclude the Dutch and English fleets from the Mediterranean ; but the Spanish dominions included further, Naples, Sicily, the Tuscan ports and the Milanese, which gave overpowering strength within that same sea. The acquisition of the Spanish Netherlands—what is now called Belgium—laid bare the southern frontier of the Dutch Netherlands, and placed them at France's mercy, while that of Ostend, Nieuport, and above all Antwerp, furnished bases for the invasion of England. Thus the Maritime Powers, as England and the United Provinces were styled, were directly menaced at home, while the addition of the vast Spanish Empire in the new world to the territory already occupied by France in North America and the West Indies threatened the extinction not only of all Dutch and English Colonies, but of their trade in the Western Hemisphere. In fact, if Louis were allowed to have his way there would be an end not only of the liberties of England, but of England herself.

William of course understood the full significance of the situation at once ; not so the wise men of the English Parliament. They were as usual divided into two factions, and were busy with the only work which they thoroughly enjoy and can perform with real efficiency, that of tearing each other's blind eyes out. This they varied with the congenial task of cutting down the numbers of the Army to dangerous weakness, for they were, with some excuse, out of temper. They had been committed to a long and costly war, in which their Dutch leader, William, had not been successful in the field, and they had before them the unpleasing prospect of paying the bill. The state of Europe was a small matter to them as compared with their own petty quarrels. Early in 1701 Louis surprised the frontier fortresses of the Spanish Netherlands, which were held by Dutch garrisons, and took fifteen thousand Dutch soldiers, the flower of their infantry, as his prisoners, only releasing them upon the recognition by the United Provinces of Philip as King of Spain. England thereupon acknowledged Philip likewise, after which she slowly began to awake to the meaning of all that was going forward. The Spanish fortresses were occupied by French soldiers; the Spanish traderoutes were patrolled by French fleets; English and Dutch traders were by French proclamation warned off from the commerce with the Levant and the Indies. Moreover, France was seconding the work of Army and Fleet by masterly diplomacy. She secured the friend-ship of Portugal, which was the only base from which Spain could be attacked by land ; of the Duchy of Savoy, which made safe the com-munications between France and Italy ; of the electorate of Bavaria, astride the Danube, which opened the road to Vienna ; and of the electorate of Cologne, which last covered the eastern flank of the Netherlands and cut the communications of Holland and England with the Upper Rhine. It was high time for England to wake up. Parliament, forgetting its quarrels, addressed the King unanimously, assuring him of its readiness to support his Allies, and voted the necessary supplies for the purpose.

III

ARMED with such powers, William at once set about the reconstruction of a Grand Alliance against France. The Emperor, being a rival claimant to the crown of Spain, was quite ready to join it, but he was hampered by the state of his finances, by a rebellion, fomented by the French, in Hungary, and by the menace of an attack by Turkey. However, he took the offensive at once, sending an army under Prince Eugene of Savoy across the Alps upon Lombardy. Denmark likewise signed a subsidiary treaty. But William, conscious of failing health, was fain to entrust negotiations with all other Powers to Marlborough. He recognised in Marlborough the one man who could take over from him the diplomatic and military direction of the coming struggle, and he was great enough to forget the past, and to trust him absolutely and completely. First, Marlborough went over to the Hague with William to build up an arrangement with the Dutch. It was no easy matter to reconcile the conflicting claims of the

23

English, the Dutch and the Emperor, whose ministers were at the Hague ; but by patience and tact Marlborough accomplished it. In the first week of September the treaty was signed. The Empire was to provide ninety thousand men, the Dutch ten thousand and England forty thousand, native soldiers or mercenaries. The treaty left an opening for other Powers to come in, if they wished, notably Denmark and Prussia ; and, since the French had been endeavouring to tamper with Sweden, Marlborough by high words and large payments succeeded in obtaining a pledge from Charles XII. to stand outside the contest or even possibly to aid the Grand Alliance with men. Infinite tact, patience and address were needed to carry these negotiations to a successful issue, yet Marlborough, except in the case of Sweden, left the last word always with the English Parliament. Sweden he bound down by his own act, for Charles XII. was a flighty genius who might change his mind ; but Marlborough knew his countrymen too well to allow them to think that their servant was their master. His difficulties at home were not less than his difficulties abroad, but he managed to surmount all the worst of them.

It is worth recording that on the 1st of

June Marlborough was appointed General of all the Foot Forces in the Kingdom—a curious limitation—and that a month later William Cadogan, whose name does not appear on the English Establishment until 1694, when he was a humble captain, was nominated Quartermaster-general. In September James II. died. Parliament had already passed an Act vesting the succession in the Protestant descendants of the Electress Sophia of Hanover; but Louis XIV. by a singular blunder recognised James II.'s son as King. Thereby he rallied to William all the partisans of the Revolution, and a general election returned a large majority of them to Parliament. Marlborough's treaties were confirmed with high approbation, and liberal supplies were voted for the increase of the Army and for other preparations for war. They were necessary, for Parliament had treated the troops so infamously after the Peace of Ryswick that recruits were reluctant to take the shilling. In February 1702 Marlborough was made Colonel of the regiment now called the South Wales Borderers, a favour which manifested William's confidence in him. A month later, on the 8th March, William died ; and Anne succeeded him on the throne. Within a fortnight she made Marlborough a

25

Knight of the Garter and Captain-General of all her forces, and sent him as Envoy Extraordinary to the Hague, there to give assurance that she intended to pursue William's policy with all possible energy. The Dutch, greatly comforted, accepted his advice as to the coming campaign, and insisted upon placing their troops under his command, to the exclusion of many royal princes, and even of one king, who were serving with the Allies. This was awkward, for Queen Anne was very anxious that her husband, Prince George of Denmark, a most incompetent person, should be Commander-in-Chief; but the Dutch were firm, and Marlborough finally accepted the place with a salary of £10,000 a year. It remained for him to arrange for the conduct of affairs at home. Diplomatic and military matters he kept in his own hands; and having received the further appointment of Master-General of the Ordnance, he was supreme not only over horse, foot and artillery, but over *matériel* as well as *personnel*. For the management of the finance he selected his son-in-law, Godolphin, the most competent man in England, and like himself a public servant rather than a politician. For the rest he tried to unite both factions for the common cause. ' I know them so well,' he wrote to his wife, ' that if my quiet depended upon either of them I should be most miserable.' Whigs, who nominally favoured the Revolution, Tories, who nominally upheld the dynasty of the Stuarts and prated of divine right, doubtless talked much of their respective causes, but thought chiefly of themselves. Marlborough himself was not free from this weakness. Few things try poor human nature so deeply as a disputed succession, an uncertainty as to masters ; and earnestly though Marlborough might strive towards a National Government, irrespective of faction, he was doomed ultimately to fail. Against human vanity and selfishness, not less than against human stupidity, the gods themselves fight in vain.

IV

It is necessary before going further to gain some idea of the conduct of war in those days. Professional armies were still a comparative novelty, and they were so costly that sovereigns were careful of hazarding them in action. They even sent civilians to check the generals lest they should be unduly rash. The great masters of the art therefore shrank from seeking a hasty decision, and sought rather to grind down their enemy by slow wear and tear. The system preferred was to invade an enemy's country, and 'subsist comfortably,' that is to say, at the enemy's expense. With this object, generals entrenched their armies to the teeth, and would sit looking at each other without daring to attack for months together. Sometimes the entire summer was spent in this way, until one side or the other was compelled to move by want of food and forage. Then the other side followed him up cautiously and sat down as before. Frequently there were complicated manœuvres by one side to tempt

28

the other to weaken the garrison of a fortress ;
and, if they were successful, the fortress was
besieged by part of the force and the siege was
covered by the remainder. Occasionally this
policy was reversed, and fortresses were threatened in order that their garrisons might be
strengthened and the field army thus weakened.
But the rule was that a pitched battle must be
avoided, unless there were enormous odds in
favour of the side that risked it. In any case,
whatever the issue of a campaign, both sides
went into winter-quarters and remained there
inactive until the next spring. During this
period of rest the officers went home and
gathered recruits to replace casualties and prepare for the next campaign. Generals really
had little choice about this. Roads were so
bad, so little ground had been drained and so
little was understood of sanitary science, that
armies would simply have melted away from
dysentery and exposure if they had tried to
continue operations through the winter. The
same dearth of roads and abundance of marsh
and forest contributed to make the feeding of
an army a difficult matter, and of a large army
—say one hundred thousand men—a most
formidable task. The favourite fighting grounds
were rich alluvial plains where crops were

heavy and foodstuffs accordingly plentiful. If such plains were watered by navigable rivers or canals, they were preferred, because of the facilities offered by water-transport for moving heavy material of war, such as a siege train. The Spanish Netherlands—Belgium—offered all of these advantages, and was accordingly one of the cockpits of Europe. So well was the ground known, and so often had it been traversed by armies, that it became a kind of chess-board on which a player could foresee with practical certainty the series of moves which would follow upon a certain opening. Its southern borders were studded with an in-finity of fortresses great and small, and engineers could predict almost to a day the length of the siege which each, under given conditions, could sustain before it surrendered. Thus insensibly there grew up in France, which was perpetually trying to enlarge its northern frontiers, the idea that sieges constituted the chief business of war. Louis xiv. in particular delighted in sieges, for he could move his Court down to the scene of action with all of its paraphernalia, not omitting a theatrical company and a court-painter, to witness the operations from a safe distance, and enjoy the pomp and triumph of the subsequent surrender. France set the military fashion in Europe ; and her ways naturally found favour with officers of all other countries. A general in those days could almost conduct war according to printed formula, especially in Belgium ; and there was a tendency to apply these formulas to all operations, whatever the theatre of war.

Now Marlborough, far ahead of his time, had no notion of conducting war in this fashion. Other men might be content to capture a few French fortresses, and feed their men and horses at French expense by occupying a few square miles of French territory. France held a central position, even as did the Central Powers in the late German war, and could act, to use the old phrase, upon interior lines. She could, therefore, play such a game with great advantage over the Allies. Marlborough's idea was to smash the French armies in the field, march straight upon Paris and obtain a rapid decision. There were only two other great soldiers, Prince Eugene of Savoy and the French Marshal Villars, who held the like views about seeking out your enemy and beating him at once. But they, even as Marlborough, were too much in advance of their generation to be understood.

Furthermore, Marlborough wished to throw

the main strength of England into the direct struggle with France upon the Continent. He was thoroughly imbued, as no French soldier has ever been, with the importance of sea-power, and, as shall be seen, was very far from neglecting it ; but he wished his main blow to be struck at the heart. Once, to change the metaphor, the trunk was felled, it would be easy to sever the branches. But here at once he fell foul of the old English prejudice which showed itself so strongly even in the late German war. Many men of influence, who had their spokesmen in the Government, wished to devote all England's energies to the capture of distant French and Spanish possessions—in fact to ' side-shows '—exactly as the younger Pitt did with such disastrous consequences in 1793.

These same individuals also maintained that, if troops were to be sent to the Continent at all, they should be sent to Spain, since the Spanish succession was the cause of the war. But they ignored the unquestionable fact that the real enemy was not Spain but France. Vanquish France, and it would be easy to deal with Spain. Invade Spain—proverbially the most difficult of all theatres of war—and it would be easy to raise up innumerable enemies there, but it would not injure France.

Marlborough, then, from the first took Paris as his main objective, and instead of entangling himself among the maze of fortresses upon the French northern frontier, purposed to establish his base at Coblenz, at the junction of the Rhine and the Moselle, and to advance upon Paris by the valley of the Moselle. For this purpose he desired first to clear the French away from the triangle between the Meuse and the Rhine, and to deprive them so far as possible of the use of both waterways. At the moment the whole line of the Rhine from Coblenz to the Dutch frontier was in the enemy's hands ; and it was essential to wrest it from them.

On the 15th of May war was formally declared by England against France, and on the 23rd Marlborough left Margate for the Hague, watching through a perspective glass (an early form of telescope) for a last sight of his beloved Sarah, and inditing her a love-letter when the cliffs faded out of view. At the Hague a thousand affairs, diplomatic and military, occupied him until the end of June, when at last he set out to take command in the field. It is not easy at this distance of time to conjure up a sight of his headquarters. His pay of £10,000 a year, worth perhaps £75,000 at the present

C   33

time, from the Dutch alone, sounds enormous, but his expenses must have been very great. As Commander-in-Chief of an army which included not a few royal and serene highnesses together with a host of the noble and the highest well-born, he had to keep up a certain amount of state and to maintain a very profuse table. The silver vessels which he took upon his campaigns, especially ' pilgrim bottles ' for the conveyance of wine, suggest that consumption of liquor (though he was himself a most temperate man) must have been very considerable. And all these heavy and valuable articles had to be watched, and packed up on waggons or pack-animals and counted in and counted out by a retinue of servants under the superintendence of stewards and controllers and what not. Altogether the number of men and animals (all with mouths to be filled) employed upon this business alone must have been formidable. Then Marlborough had with him his coach—we know it because he put Tallard into it after Blenheim—with at least six horses, to say nothing of spare harness horses and his own riding horses. Next, apart from what may be called the household, there was the Staff proper, with Cadogan, the indefatigably diligent and invariably courteous, at its head, and

34

an uncertain number of deputies and assistants of many tongues and nations, exchanging ideas in bad French. Then there was the Secretary, not a military but a general secretary, Adam Cardonnel, the Huguenot, whose French was presumably correct, with his clerks, and all the records of headquarters, demanding more horses and more waggons. The daily cost of all this to the Commander-in-Chief must have been immense ; and even so, no money was allowed by any State for the purchase of intelligence. The contractor for bread and bread-waggons paid by established usage a percentage upon his contract to the Commander-in-Chief for this purpose, and no doubt made allowance for it when the agreement was drawn up. Marlborough himself, so far as we know, was never seen abroad without the great wig which had replaced the long curls of his youth, gold-laced hat, and scarlet gold-laced coat crossed by the blue ribbon of the Garter. Working in his office after the active tasks of the day were over, he probably replaced the wig with a white linen cap, and the scarlet coat and riding-boots with a loose gown and shoes. Portentous though his correspondence was, he himself hated writing unless it were perpetual love-letters to his Sarah.

35

V

THE campaign of 1702 had begun in the ortho-
dox way. There were detachments of the
French and of the Allies watching each other
on the Upper Rhine, the Lower Rhine and
the Lower Scheldt ; but the grand French
Army under Marshal Boufflers, sixty thousand
strong, lay in the territory of Cleve, subsisting
comfortably at the expense of Prussia, whose
property Cleve was. The French had seized
every fortress on the Meuse, except Maastricht,
from Namur to Venloo, so that they were
practically masters of that important waterway.
Over against Boufflers and about twenty miles
from him lay twenty-five thousand men under
the Dutch General Ginkell, watching him
anxiously under shelter of three fortresses which
barred the way into the Dutch Netherlands by
the way of the Rhine and Meuse. On the 10th
of June, Boufflers had made a dash to cut Ginkell off from his central fortress of Nimeguen ;
and Ginkell had only escaped by a headlong
retreat. All Holland quivered with fright ; and

36

remained quivering until on the 2nd of July Marlborough arrived at Nimeguen, attended by two Dutch civilian deputies to see that he did nothing imprudent with the Dutch troops.

Rapidly he concentrated sixty thousand men, only twelve thousand of them British, and moved to within two leagues of Boufflers, when the Dutch deputies became frightened and insisted on delay. At last they allowed him to cross to the left bank of the Meuse. ' Now,' he said to the Dutch deputies on the 26th of July, ' I shall soon rid you of your troublesome neighbours.' Five swift marches southward brought him across the line of the French communications with the Spanish Netherlands, and Boufflers, hastily breaking up his camp, crossed the Meuse and hurried northward likewise. By the 2nd of August the two armies had converged to within striking distance, Marlborough's fresh, ready and confident, Boufflers' weary and dismayed. Marlborough was for an immediate attack ; but the Dutch deputies interposed, and a certain victory was thrown away. Keeping his temper, Marlborough said nothing, and allowed Boufflers to retire safely to the Spanish Netherlands. Then, using a convoy as a bait, he tempted Boufflers to move northward once more, and once again slipped in between him and the frontier. On the 22nd of August he had the French at his mercy, entangled in difficult ground and in confusion. This time Marlborough gave the order to attack, but a Dutch general, Opdam, who commanded ten thousand men, refused to move, and a second great chance was thrown away. There was still good prospect of success by an attack on the following day, but the Dutch deputies intervened, and a third great opportunity was sacrificed. Still Marlborough made no public complaint ; but the troops were not deceived and loudly denounced both Dutch deputies and Dutch generals. In the circumstances Marlborough decided to devote the rest of the campaign to the recovery of the fortresses on the Meuse. These fell rapidly one after another, and Marlborough resolved to finish the series by the capture of Liège. The Dutch deputies hesitated, fearing that Boufflers might risk a battle to save it. Boufflers as a matter of fact did move out, but found Marlborough awaiting him with a superior force. For the fourth time Marlborough saw victory within his grasp, and for the fourth time the Dutch deputies refused to allow their troops to attack. Boufflers hurried back to the protection of fortified lines in Brabant, and Liège presently fell. There-

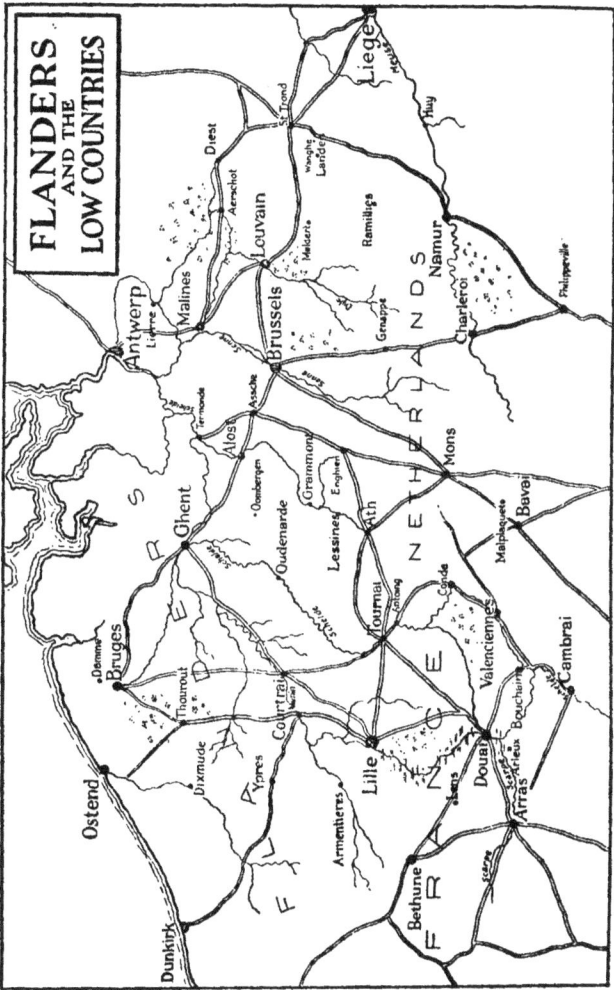

FLANDERS
AND THE
LOW COUNTRIES

with at the end of October the campaign came to a close. For any other general it would have been considered a marvellous achievement. For Marlborough it was a sickening failure. All of his plans had been wrecked by Dutch jealousy and Dutch stupidity.

The troops went into winter-quarters, and Marlborough himself started for the Hague by water down the Meuse in company with some Dutch officers. It was a custom of the time that officers should receive passports from the enemy at the close of operations; and the whole party, except Marlborough, possessed such passports. On the journey the escort went astray, and the boat was captured by a roving band of the French. Marlborough was not recognised, and by good fortune his servant had a passport made out for Marlborough's brother, General Charles Churchill, which he slipped into his master's hand. Marlborough presented it with his usual serenity and was allowed to go on his way; but the rumour of his capture spread far and wide; and when he reached the Hague the whole population came out to welcome him, men and women weeping for joy and kissing even his boots and his horse.

Upon his return to England in December, the Queen announced that she intended to promote him to be Marquis of Blandford and Duke of Marlborough. Sarah, his wife, demurred to this, dreading the outcry of the jealous, and arguing truly that he had not the fortune to maintain so great a position. The Queen thereupon offered a pension of £5000, but Sarah still protested, and Marlborough agreed with her except upon one point. The step in rank would greatly increase his influence and authority upon the Continent and so make easier the delicate duties of command. Wholly upon public grounds, therefore, he accepted the dukedom, but declined an additional pension of £2000 a year from the Queen's privy purse. So much has been said of his ambition and his avarice that these facts must be set down.

In Parliament he found, of course, the usual factions and struggles continuing with all their old vigour, but there was no obstruction to the maintenance of the Army. As regards the general military situation, things had not on the whole gone ill in 1702. An English expedition, originally projected by King William, and approved by Marlborough, against Cadiz, the centre of Spanish trade with the new world, had failed owing to the incompetence of the commanders ; but by good luck they had captured the Spanish treasure-fleet on their

way home ; and the general result had been
to secure the transfer of Portugal to the side
of the Allies. There was hope, therefore, that
the despatch of a fleet to the Mediterranean
might secure also the defection of Savoy from
the party of France. On the other hand, to the
east of the Rhine—that is to say in the direction of the Empire—the French and their Allies
had made solid progress. The Elector of
Bavaria had seized the vital position of Ulm and
had opened communication with the French
on the Upper Rhine. Villars, who commanded the French in that quarter, had beaten
his Imperialist opponent at Friedlingen and
cleared the passage of the Black Forest, and
Tallard had taken Trèves and Trarbach on
the Moselle. This was serious ; but worse
was to come. Throwing all rules to the winds,
Villars collected his astonished troops and disgusted officers from their winter-quarters at
Strassburg in January 1703, marched them
fifty miles up the Rhine to the nearest bridge,
crossed the river, marched down again under
the very guns of the Imperialist fortresses to
Kehl, besieged and captured the place within
twelve days, and by the middle of March stood
ready, with the bridge of Kehl in his possession, to penetrate the mountains and join the

Elector of Bavaria, possibly for a march upon Vienna itself.

Such was the general position when Marlborough left England for the Hague in March 1703. He was a very sad man, for he had just lost his only son, a most promising boy of seventeen, from smallpox, and had left his wife behind him almost distracted by grief. He found little to comfort him among the Dutch. He wished to counter the thrust of Villars towards the Empire by the invasion of Brabant and the capture of Antwerp and Ostend ; but the Dutch were far too timid to favour such an adventure. They insisted upon the siege of Bonn, a pointless operation, which Marlborough undertook in order to conciliate them. He of course achieved the task with swift success, but his greater project was brought to naught by the perversity of the Dutch generals and the vacillation of the Dutch Government. It would be tedious to go into detail. It must suffice to say that for eighteen days Marlborough's army lay within striking distance of the French ; that every day he entreated for permission to attack, and every day pleaded in vain. The campaign of the Allies in 1703 was utterly thrown away in passive safeguarding of the Dutch frontier.

43

VI

MEANWHILE the situation on the side of the Empire had become more serious. Villars had advanced through the Black Forest, joined hands with the Elector of Bavaria, and in combination with him had beaten the Imperialists at Hochstädt. The Elector and the French, now under Marsin, were masters of the line of the Danube from Ulm to Linz, and were working in combination with the Hungarian rebels, who were threatening desolation almost to the walls of Vienna. Moreover, they were supported in the Upper Rhine by forty-five thousand men under Tallard, who had fought a successful campaign in that quarter, and while neutralising the Imperial forces which opposed him there, could afford to send reinforcements to Marsin. Unless the Allies could move to the assistance of the Emperor on his own ground he was lost. It was too late to think of saving him by a counter-stroke against Paris, even if the Dutch and Germans could have been brought to consent to such a project. Paris

44

could hardly be reached, under the most favourable conditions, until 1705, whereas Vienna,
unless succoured, must fall in 1704. And with
the fall of Vienna the coalition of the Allies
would inevitably be dissolved.

Prince Eugene, who was at the head of the
Imperial Military Council, had long been in
correspondence with Marlborough on the sub-
ject, and the two had agreed that an offensive
movement from the Rhine upon the Danube
alone could save the Empire. But the enterprise must be prepared with the utmost secrecy
and the Allies must somehow be induced to
take part in it. This was Marlborough's business, and the most difficult portion of it. Affairs
in Parliament were not in too satisfactory a
state, for faction was increasingly busy and
the unsatisfactory issue of the last campaign
might well provoke discontent. But the supplies
for the war, including an additional ten thousand men, were duly voted ; and in January
1704, for there was no time to be lost, Marlborough crossed the North Sea in bitter weather
to Holland.

There he began work with consummate address. For the coming campaign he put forward his favourite design of an advance on
Paris by the Moselle ; for this would involve

45

concentrations of the Army at Coblenz, and Coblenz as a base would serve as well for advance to the Danube as towards Paris. He communicated his project secretly to the King of Prussia, who, greatly flattered, promised an augmentation of his troops in the field. Prince Louis of Baden, the very wooden officer who had been matched with dismal unsuccess against the French on the Upper Rhine, sent Marlborough a plan of his own for operations on the Moselle ; and Marlborough answered that it would be the very thing for him. The Dutch were more troublesome. They declared that they would spare no troops outside their own frontiers. Marlborough said flatly that in that case he would march without them ; and the Dutch gave in. Marlborough was careful to leave the native Dutch behind, and to take only the foreign regiments in Dutch pay, whereby he rid himself of the curse of Dutch deputies. There were ten thousand things to be thought of and provided for—new shoes to replace those worn out on the march for one item, peaceful passage through the territory of petty potentates for another—and all to be done without provoking suspicion of the real design. At last in May the Army was assembled at Bedburg, about thirty miles west of Cologne, where on the 18th of May Marlborough joined them. It numbered under forty thousand men, including sixteen thousand British, but was to be joined by other troops from the Rhine as it moved on. A fortnight earlier he had admitted Sarah to his secret. ' I am going up into Germany where it would be impossible for you to follow me ; but love me as you now do and no hurt can come to me.'

The French dispositions were not calculated to disturb Marlborough. One army of forty thousand men under Marshal Villeroi lay on the eastern border of the Spanish Netherlands ; another under Tallard was about Strassburg ; ten thousand men were on the Moselle ready to act in Flanders or in Germany as required ; and lastly, at Ulm lay the forty-five thousand men under the Elector of Bavaria and Marsin, awaiting only reinforcements from Tallard to march on Vienna. It was the business of Prince Louis of Baden to prevent the passage of this reinforcement if he could, but he was more concerned with the safety of his own territory than with any other matter, and Tallard pushed ten thousand men through the Black Forest without molestation. The French had scored the first point in the game.

Meanwhile Marlborough on the 19th of May

had started upon his famous march, pointing
first up the Rhine to Coblenz. On the very
first day he received shrieks of alarm from rear
and front. The Dutch announced that Villeroi
was astir, and entreated him to come back ;
Prince Louis of Baden reported that Tallard
was on the move, and urged him to hasten
forward. Such are the ways of generals in
a Grand Alliance. Marlborough calmed the
nerves of both parties by judicious messages
and orders, and went his own way. Starting
always at dawn and bringing his troops into
camp at noon, he himself rode ahead with his
cavalry, left the infantry and artillery to follow,
and granted his troopers no halt until they had
crossed the Rhine at Coblenz and reached the
ground over against Mainz on the 29th of May.
Here, with a few final feints to convince the
French that his designs still lay on the Moselle,
he struck rapidly south and east, and so passed
beyond their reach. On the 9th of June he
reached Mundelsheim, about twenty-five miles
north and west of Stuttgart, where he halted
for three days to allow the infantry to come up ;
and now for the first time he met Eugene in
the flesh.

He found a spare man of middle height, with
a meagre face, large nose, bright brown eyes

under eyebrows that tilted upwards towards the temples, and a long firm chin. Grandson of Charles Emmanuel I., Duke of Savoy, Eugene had been born in Paris in 1663 and had been destined for the Church. Preferring a military career, he had asked Louis XIV. for a regiment and had been refused. Therewith he had carried his sword to the Emperor Leopold and become the sworn enemy of France. Employed in several campaigns against the Turks, he had through sheer merit risen before he was thirty to be Commander-in-Chief, and in 1697 had dealt the Turks a decisive blow at the battle of Zenta. Intrigue at the Court of Vienna had caused him to be coldly received after this great service ; but his merit was so great that he was able to make his own terms when his employers again sought his help, and thus he obtained a free hand in the direction of all future campaigns. Since 1701 he had been for two years fighting the French in Italy and latterly the Hungarian insurgents ; and now here he was, the right man in the right place at the right time. Rather cold and severe in character, he must have made a good foil to the grace and charm of Marlborough, but he knew a great man when he saw him. He was a great snuff-taker, and we may guess that he emptied pocketsful of snuff in satisfaction while he listened to the good sense of Marlborough's bad French.

The Prince inspected the English horse, and was astonished at the condition of men and animals after so long and trying a march. Marlborough, like Wellington, was evidently a good horsemaster. But Eugene was especially struck by the appearance of the men. ' I have heard much,' he said, ' of the English cavalry, and find it to be the best appointed and finest that I have ever seen. The spirit which I see in the looks of your men is an earnest of victory.' Unfortunately, three days later there appeared a less welcome colleague, Prince Louis of Baden. Marlborough would fain have kept Eugene with him, but it was finally decided that Eugene should take Prince Louis's place on the Rhine, to prevent Tallard, if possible, from crossing the river and to follow him at all hazards if he should succeed in crossing ; while Prince Louis should remain in charge of Eugene's Austrian troops, sharing the command with Marlborough on alternate days. It was as though Fabius should command on alternate days with Scipio.

The march was resumed on the 14th of June, and the troops entered the mountain-chain

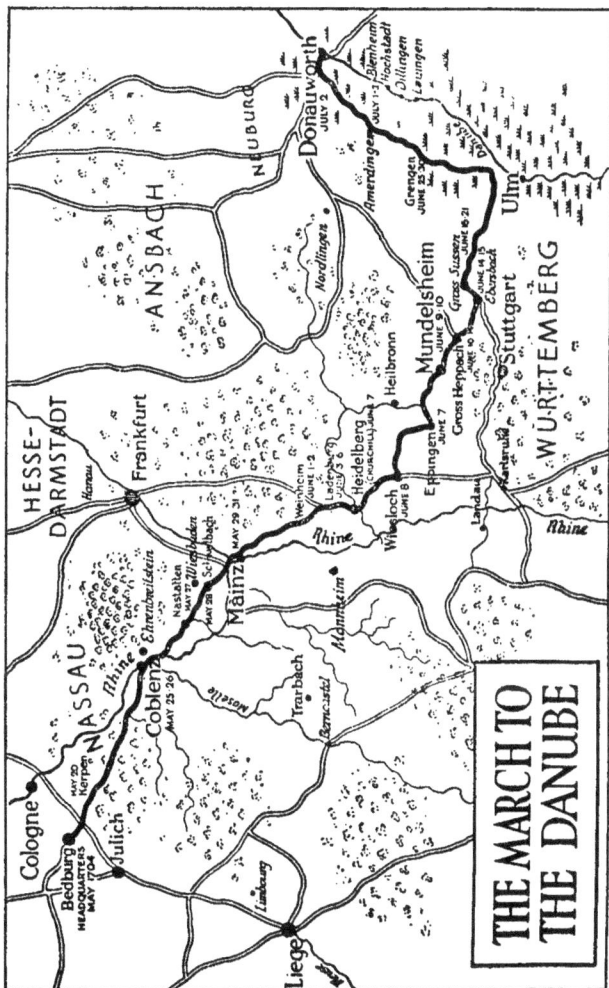

THE MARCH TO THE DANUBE

that bounds the valley of the Danube. The rain fell incessantly and the roads were in a terrible state ; and now once again Marlborough was troubled by a panic message from the Dutch, imploring the return of their auxiliary troops. He calmed their troubled spirits by ordering boats to be ready to carry the Dutch auxiliaries down the Rhine, but was careful to lead the auxiliaries themselves onwards towards Ulm. On the 22nd of June he effected his junction with the Imperialist troops under Prince Louis of Baden, and on the 25th the united forces were within eight miles of Ulm. Thereupon the Elector of Bavaria withdrew his army to an impregnable position between Lauingen and Dillingen, on the north bank of the Danube, midway between Ulm and Donauwörth. The Allies then turned northward to await the arrival of the British infantry at Gingen.

Marlborough's brother, Charles Churchill, had had terrible struggles to bring forward the infantry and artillery in perpetual pouring rain. The ascent even of a single hill in that mountainous country often occupied the artillery for a day, and would frequently have taken still longer but for the extraordinary exertions of the officers. The men naturally suffered much hardship, but bore it with patience, knowing that they were not forgotten by their chief. Marlborough's solicitude for their welfare and discipline was incessant. He had foreseen and provided for all their wants, not omitting the most important detail of shoes. He was merciless to all plunderers, but took care to pay the men regularly so that they could honestly purchase everything that they needed. Such a thing had never before been known in a German campaign. Yet Marlborough desired something more than merely to leave a friendly population in his rear, important though that might be. He aimed also at heightening the self-respect of his troops, and he succeeded. The behaviour of the British, amid many trials, was exemplary.

VII

MARLBOROUGH's objective from the first had been Donauwörth, the possession of which would give him at once a bridge over the Danube, and a place of arms for the invasion of Bavaria. Its fortifications were obsolete, but nearly half of its perimeter was covered by the Danube and the remainder was dominated by a steep and lofty hill called the Bell-Hill or Schellenberg, with a plateau on its summit which would hold twenty thousand men. The fortification of this hill by earthworks had already been begun, the entrenchments running up from the very ditch of the fortress to the top. Thus on the slope most accessible to attack the assaulting columns would be exposed to enfilading fire from the walls of Donauwörth as well as to direct fire from the front. Altogether the Schellenberg was a formidable stronghold ; yet it must be taken, and taken at once before Villeroi and Tallard should arrive with the French army from the Rhine. Moreover, the capture of Donauwörth and the

54

mastery of the bridge would threaten the Elector's communications and compel him to retire from his impregnable position.

On the 30th of June and the following day the Allied army made two marches which brought it within fifteen miles of Donauwörth. The Elector, watching the movement from the opposite bank of the Danube, responded by sending a strong detachment of all three arms to reinforce the Schellenberg and hasten the work of entrenchment. On the 2nd of July it was Marlborough's turn to command. Before daylight Cadogan set out with an advanced party, and at 3 a.m. Marlborough in person marched with a picked body of about eight thousand foot and three thousand horse ; the main body of the army following two hours later. By 9 a.m. Marlborough had joined Cadogan, but the enemy took no alarm, for a fortified position supported by the artillery of a fortress was deemed by all rules to be un-assailable. Moreover, no enemy after a long march would dream of attempting to storm it with weary troops. Not until the afternoon did the commandant on the Schellenberg awake to his danger, when he made sound dispositions, posting eight of his fifteen guns at the angle of the entrenchments remotest from the

55

fortress. Here also, as the point of assault that
would probably be chosen by an enemy, he
stationed the bulk and the best of his infantry.
It was 4 p.m. before Marlborough could form
his columns of attack, the roads being so bad
that the infantry had taken eight hours to
traverse fifteen miles. Meanwhile the cavalry
was set to cut fascines, and while this was going
forward a letter reached Marlborough from
Eugene to the effect that Villeroi and Tallard
were preparing to send strong reinforcements
to the Elector. Only the advanced detachment was yet on the ground, but there was no
time to be lost, for Prince Louis of Baden would
be in command next day and might shrink from
the risk of attack. Sixteen battalions, five of
them British, were drawn up in four lines,
with eight more in support, and the cavalry
were drawn up in two lines behind them. Eight
more battalions were held in reserve. General
Goor, an able and gallant Dutchman, was in
command of the whole. At 6 p.m. Marlborough gave the word to advance. Two
parties of British grenadiers from the First
Guards led the way under Colonel Munden
and Lord Mordaunt, and the hostile batteries
in Donauwörth and on the Schellenberg opened
a cross-fire of round shot. Such a fire was one

of the greatest trials of the old warfare. The round shot ricochetted along the ground like cricket balls, sometimes apparently so harmless that men had been known to lose a leg by putting out a foot to stop them. These shot could be plainly seen coming, and yet a man might not move out of their way. Many troops could not endure the ordeal, but the British would always face it, and now they set the example to the rest. The grenadiers pressed on to within eighty yards of the entrenchment before they fired a shot ; and then the enemy, excellent Bavarian infantry and artillery, opened upon them with musketry and grape-shot :— grape-shot, the old substitute for the modern machine gun, very deadly up to two hundred yards, and with a terrifying whistle which shook irresolute soldiers. Goor was shot dead almost immediately. Few of the grenadiers were left standing. Mordaunt with his skirts torn to shreds and Munden with his hat riddled to fragments by bullets kept waving the remnant on. Then the columns reached a hollow road, and mistaking it for the ditch of the entrenchment, threw down their fascines to traverse it. Presently they reached the ditch itself, found it impassable, wavered and began to fall back. The gallant Bavarians sprang out to counter-attack with the bayonet. Most of the Allied troops gave way, but the First Guards, Royal Scots and Royal Welch stood firm, and after desperate fighting the Bavarians were driven back into their lines.

The Allied columns were quickly re-formed, and the attack was renewed, with terrible loss but with no better success. The storming columns fell back in disorder, and were only checked by the British cavalry under General Lumley, which moved forward into the fire and formed a rallying point. Some of the attacking troops, however, swerving towards Donauwörth, found that the entrenchment near the ditch of the fortress was but weakly held. The news was passed to the main body, which was now approaching, and Prince Louis of Baden, leading his troops forward, mastered that part of the entrenchment with ease and moved them up against the flank of the defenders. The commandant on the Schellenberg tried to parry the stroke by a charge of nine French and Bavarian squadrons, but these were shivered to pieces by the fire of the Imperialist infantry. The fugitive horse fled into Donauwörth, kindling such a panic that the place was instantly surrendered. Marlborough meanwhile had been re-forming the columns for a third

58

attack, and had dismounted the Scots Greys to take part in it. But just then the Bavarians, becoming aware of the threat to their flank, began to waver. The columns of the frontal attack sprang forward ; and the defenders, who had hitherto carried themselves with noble gallantry, fled headlong as a disorderly mob. The Greys remounted, and with the rest of the Allied cavalry rushed forward to the chase. The fighting had been savage and the pursuit was ruthless. A few fugitives escaped by swimming the Danube, but more were drowned. It was reckoned that of ten to twelve thousand men who had held the Schellenberg, not more than three thousand rejoined the Elector.

The whole affair had lasted little more than an hour and a half, and in that short space there fell of the Allies five thousand four hundred killed and wounded, including no fewer than seventeen general officers. Prince Louis of Baden, a brave soldier if no great commander, was himself among the hurt. The honours of the day rested with the British, whose casualties numbered fifteen hundred—a far greater proportion than that of any other contingent—and both sides agreed that the British had set a new standard of valour. Of the First Guards five officers only out of seventeen were unhurt, and among these five, marvellous to say, were both Mordaunt and Munden ; but of the eighty-two grenadiers whom they led to the assault only twenty-one returned. In fact the casualty list would have seemed heavy even in the twentieth century. But the prize was worth the sacrifice. Marlborough had played for a big stake, but he had won. Not another general in Europe, with the possible exception of Eugene, would have ventured upon so daring a stroke ; and the moral effect was immense. Here was a leader who had marched from the North Sea to the Danube while three hostile armies stood looking on in helpless bewilderment, and had at its close let fall a crushing blow. The Elector's finest regiments were ruined ; the prestige of France was shaken ; and the confidence of the Allies was immensely enhanced. The 2nd of July 1704 was a very great day.

VIII

THE Elector at once retreated with Marsin in company, and entrenched himself under the guns of Augsburg. Marlborough, after three days spent in disposing of his wounded and looking to his magazines, crossed the Danube on the 5th, and moving south-eastward halted over against Augsburg on the eastern bank of the Leck, effectually barring the road to Vienna. The Elector's entrenched camp being impregnable, the Allied commanders had no alternative but to try to starve him out of it ; and for three weeks Bavaria was devastated in order, as Marlborough said, to deprive the enemy as well of present subsistence as of future support on this side. Marlborough, as his letters show, hated this destruction of a fair country ; and he consented to it in no spirit of wanton mischief, but for the furtherance of purely military aims. Had not reinforcements presently reached him from the Rhine, the Elector would within less than another fortnight have been starved out or compelled to fight, with the certainty of defeat.

But meanwhile Tallard had crossed the Rhine with twenty-six thousand men on the 2nd of July, and moving along the south bank of the Danube effected his junction with the Elector and Marsin on the 6th of August. Eugene, with an inferior force, followed him along the northern bank, and on the same day reached Hochstädt, about twelve miles up the river from Donauwörth. Marlborough, fully apprised of Tallard's movements, decided to move back towards the Danube, and began his march on the 4th upon Neuburg. Eugene rode out to visit him ; and it was agreed that Prince Louis of Baden should besiege Ingolstadt, about thirty miles down the river from Donauwörth and ten miles below Neuburg, with fifteen thousand men, while the rest of the army should cover the siege. Prince Louis accordingly marched on the 9th, and thus was happily got out of the way. Since the Franco-Bavarian army was united on the south bank of the Danube and the Allies were divided between both banks, the situation demanded boldness and rapidity of resolution.

Eugene had hardly left Marlborough's quarters after the departure of Prince Louis on the 9th when he returned with the news that the French and Bavarians were marching for the bridge of Dillingen, five miles above Hochstädt and thirty miles above Donauwörth, with the evident intention of overwhelming Eugene's small force, or, failing that, of attacking Marlborough's magazines at Donauwörth and to north of it. After consultation it was agreed that Eugene should fall back forthwith upon Münster, Marlborough reinforcing him at once with a strong body of cavalry and joining him with the main army as soon as possible. On the 10th the Franco-Bavarian army crossed the Danube, and Eugene looked forward to the certainty of being attacked on the morrow. But the enemy made no movement, and soon after nightfall of the 11th Marlborough's whole army had united with Eugene. It had marched twenty-four miles over bad roads and crossed three rivers in twenty hours.

The men were too much fatigued to fight on the 12th, so Marlborough and Eugene rode out to examine the enemy's position, five miles away from their own camp. They found it to be sufficiently strong, facing to the north and aligned for four miles along a gentle ridge which sloped down to a little brook called the Nebel, a sluggish water that crept between boggy banks to the Danube. The right rested on the Danube, within two hundred yards of

which stood the village of Blindheim or Blenheim, where were Tallard's headquarters. His
army covered about two miles of front, and to
the left of it stood Marsin's French, with the
village of Oberglauheim in their centre. The
forces of Tallard and Marsin, though really one
French army, were treated as two distinct units,
which can hardly have been an advantage ;
though it is said that they were kept apart lest
horse-sickness, which was raging in one of them,
should infect the other. Lastly, to left of Marsin
were the Elector's troops with their left resting
on the village of Lutzingen. The Franco-
Bavarian commanders were perfectly at their
ease. They had come down upon Marlborough
and Eugene in superior force, barring their way
up the Danube, and according to all rules they
had thereby won the campaign. Marlborough,
in their opinion, had now no choice but to re-
cross the Danube and make his way back to
the Rhine as speedily as possible. It never
occurred to them that he might make a frontal
attack against an enemy strongly posted and
superior in numbers.

They could hardly believe their eyes, therefore, when they saw the Allies advancing in
eight columns upon the morning of the 13th ;
but they made their dispositions with under-

standing. The space between the river and
Blenheim was blocked by a leaguer of waggons,
and sixteen battalions were posted in Blenheim
village itself, with eleven more in rear. From
thence almost to Oberglauheim Tallard extended two lines of horse, with a third line of
nine battalions of infantry in rear of them.
Marsin's cavalry joined the left of Tallard's,
stretching to Oberglauheim and beyond it,
while fourteen battalions occupied Oberglauheim itself. Thence the array was prolonged
by seventeen battalions of infantry, carried on
to Lutzingen by fifty-one more squadrons of
horse, and ended by nine battalions of infantry,
which were thrown back to meet a possible
flanking attack. The entire host of the Franco-
Bavarians numbered fifty-six thousand men with
ninety-two guns.

Meanwhile the Allied army was beginning
its deployment, Eugene taking the right of the
line over against the space between Oberglauheim and Lutzingen, and Marlborough the
left from Blenheim to Oberglauheim. Marlborough's troops, being nearest to the field, of
course were the first to deploy. They formed
four lines of infantry, the first and third of them
British, opposite to Blenheim ; and from Blenheim to Oberglauheim stood a line of infantry

in front, backed by two lines of cavalry in rear, and a fourth line of infantry in rear of all. On their right stood Eugene's infantry in two lines, and on their right again his cavalry faced Lutzingen. The Allies numbered in all fifty-two thousand with fifty-two guns ; so that they were matched against odds which few men would have accepted for a frontal attack.

The ordering of such an alignment was a long and tedious business, Eugene's troops having intricate and difficult ground to traverse ; and the French batteries opening fire soon after 8 a.m. did not make matters easier. Marlborough posted every one of his own batteries himself, and they replied with effect in proportion to their numbers, but Eugene could not quickly bring his guns into action. So the forenoon wore wearily away, the Allies enduring that severest of trials, total inaction under heavy fire of artillery. The chaplains came forward and read prayers at the head of each regiment, for men were not afraid to pray in those days, and Marlborough rode up and down the front of the line to give his men confidence. So, in like circumstances a century and a half later, Lord Raglan was to ride up and down his line in the full blast of the cannon-shot at the Alma. A shell burst close to Marlborough's horse, and

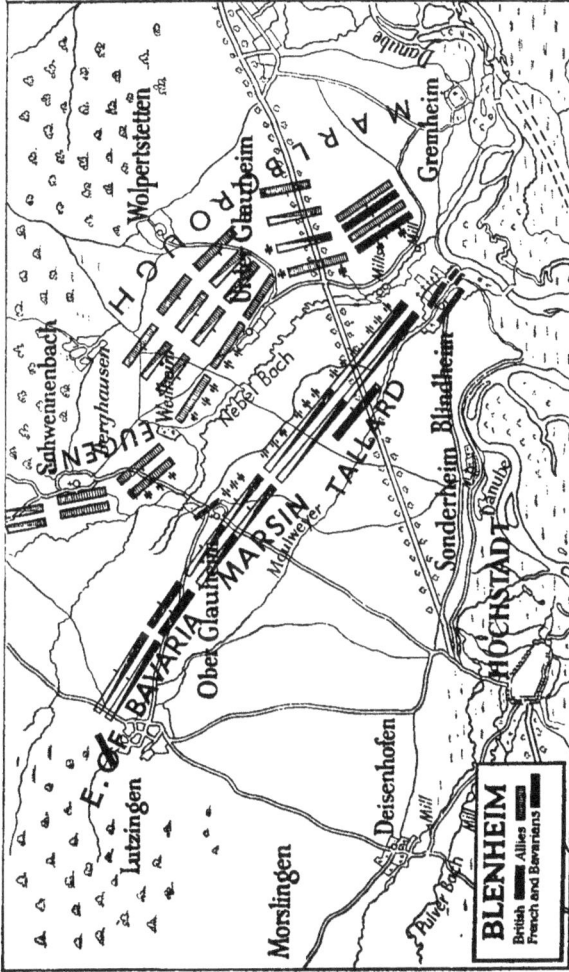

BLENHEIM
British ▬ /Allies
French and Bavarians ▬

the army held its breath as its leader vanished in a cloud of dust and smoke. But presently he emerged unhurt, his horse no doubt capering with fright, but the rider in his red coat and blue ribbon unchangeably confident and serene.

Marlborough's plan was of the nature of a tactical surprise. The boggy ground about the Nebel in his front seemed so hopelessly unfavourable to any attack of cavalry that the enemy would never expect such a stroke; and he therefore determined that he would cross the quagmire with an overwhelming mass of horse, despite of all obstacles, break through Tallard's centre and left, and cut the Franco-Bavarian army in two. This was the explanation of his unusual line of battle, which puzzled Tallard exceedingly. The first line of infantry was to cover the passage of the two lines of cavalry, and the fourth line of infantry was to support them in case of mishap. An essential part of the plan was to alarm Tallard as to the safety of his right and to induce him to weaken his centre and left; and accordingly, while the engineers were laying five pontoon-bridges over the Nebel, General Cutts, known as the Salamander from his love of a hot fire, was massing his columns for an attack upon Blenheim.

Meanwhile Eugene's army, encumbered by

difficult ground, was still toiling under a blazing sun to its appointed place. Hour after hour passed away ; messenger after messenger sped from Marlborough to Eugene with anxious enquiries ; and the hostile artillery never ceased a destructive fire. At last, at 12.30, all was ready. Cutts had backed his four lines of infantry with two lines of horse in rear. The first line was an English brigade of five battalions under General Row, who had given orders that not a shot must be fired until he struck his sword into the palisades that surrounded Blenheim. The redcoats came down to a ford of the Nebel ; and at the mere sight of them the commandant in Blenheim lost his head, and summoned the eleven battalions in rear of the village to join the sixteen within it—the very thing that Marlborough most desired. After passing the water the English came under heavy fire of grape-shot, but with Row dismounted at their head they pressed on heedless of their losses, until Row's sword fell upon the palisades. Then, pouring in one volley, they rushed forward and tried to drag down the pales by main force. In a few minutes a third of the brigade had fallen. Row was mortally wounded. The lieutenant-colonel and major of his regiment (the Royal Scots Fusiliers) were killed in an attempt to bring him off. The red-coats, shattered to pieces, fell back in disorder, and to make matters worse, three squadrons of the French gendarmerie—a very famous corps—came down upon their flank. These, however, pursuing their advantage too far, were repulsed by the second line of infantry—Hessians—and Cutts then asked for cavalry to protect his flank. Lumley sent five English squadrons, which with great difficulty struggled across the swamp, and were no sooner formed than they were confronted by eight squadrons of gendarmerie, which opened fire on them with musquetoons from the saddle. The English promptly charged them with the sword and drove them off, but pursuing, came under heavy fire and were charged in turn by fresh squadrons from Tallard's right, which drove them back to the shelter of the Hessian infantry.

Cutts now brought forward the rest of his foot, and Row's brigade, having rallied, advanced together with another English brigade once again upon Blenheim. They carried the outskirts of the village but could penetrate no further. Thrice they strove to gain more ground, and thrice they were repulsed with heavy loss. Marlborough, judging that the commandant in Blenheim was now sufficiently frightened, withdrew Cutts's infantry into some dead ground in front of the village and ordered them to keep up a constant fire with inter- mittent feints of attack. He also had the audacity to carry off one of Cutts's Hanoverian brigades to the centre, feeling confident that the enemy would not venture upon a counter- attack.

During the struggle about Blenheim, Marl- borough's main body had been fully occupied in making its way across the Nebel. The in- fantry, with the help of planks and fascines, managed to traverse the morass with compara- tively little difficulty and formed up on the other side. But any one who has observed the conditions to which even a comparatively small hunting field can reduce a piece of soft ground may imagine the flounderings of the cavalry. However, some riding, others leading their horses, they contrived to scramble across some- how ; and the English squadrons leading the way advanced through the intervals of the covering infantry upon Tallard's line of horse. They were charged and driven back by some French squadrons to the shelter of their in- fantry ; and the French were then charged in turn by fresh squadrons of the Allies, and hunted to the very rear of Tallard's position, until the Allies were forced in turn to retire by

71

the fire of musketry from Blenheim. All of this was regarded by Tallard as unworthy of serious notice. He was quite ready to allow Marlborough's troopers to advance across the morass, in order that he might drive them back into it with the greater disaster.

Marsin acted upon a different principle. He charged the Allied cavalry while still in disorder after passing the stream, and gave it no opportunity to advance. Moreover, when the first two battalions of the Allied infantry came forward to the attack of Oberglauheim they were promptly counter-attacked by nine battalions and annihilated. Following up their success, the French essayed a counter-stroke which threatened to pierce the Allied centre. Marlborough hastened to the scene of danger with the Hanoverian brigade which he had withdrawn from Cutts, and engaged the French infantry with inferior numbers, while begging Eugene earnestly for a reinforcement of cavalry. Eugene himself was in no very favourable situation. His infantry had been repulsed in a gallant attempt upon Lutzingen, and his cavalry had been roughly handled in two successive attacks ; and Marlborough's message reached him at a most critical moment. But without a thought for himself he sent at once a body of cuirassiers, which arrived in the nick of time to foil Marsin's counter-stroke. Marsin's troops fell back to Oberglauheim, where Marlborough kept them in check, as at Blenheim, by constant feint attacks.

The Duke then returned to his own left centre. It was now 4 p.m., and the whole of his cavalry was across the Nebel drawn up in two lines, with the front line of infantry transferred to the rear. He presently gave the order for this cavalry to advance, and Tallard, dismayed by its numbers and the steadiness of its array, called up his only remaining reserve, the nine battalions which stood behind his centre. Marlborough's officers promptly brought forward three German battalions and artillery to meet them ; but the nine battalions, though all of them young soldiers, stood firm for a time, and actually checked the advance of the Allies. Tallard thought that the battle was won ; and a resolute charge of his cavalry might perhaps have won it. But the French horse hung back, and the Allies recovering themselves pressed on at a trot. The French horse gave way ; Marlborough's horse gathering impetus swept on, rode down the nine battalions, and carried everything before them ; Marsin, finding his right flank laid bare, attempted to change front, but

73

he too was in difficulties, for Eugene's Prussian infantry by desperate fighting were forcing back the Elector's extreme left at Lutzingen, and Marsin was beginning to feel the pressure. In rear of his main position Tallard rallied some of his broken squadrons, but they fled again as their pursuers approached and galloped head-long down a steep descent into the marshes of the Danube. Many were drowned, and those that fled along the bank were relentlessly chased. Tallard himself, galloping towards Blenheim to give orders there, was taken prisoner, and all control of his army came to an end.

It was now past 7 p.m., and Marsin and the Elector were already in full retreat. They had set fire to Lutzingen and Oberglauheim to cover their retirement, which was rapid and orderly ; but had they not been mistaken in the failing light for Eugene's troops they would have been attacked in flank and severely pun-ished. They therefore escaped, but there re-mained still the garrison of Blenheim, which had promptly been surrounded after the defeat of Tallard's centre. A fifth assault of the Allies carried them further into the village, but failed to master it. However, several houses caught fire, and the French, miserably overcrowded in so small a place, became restive. They could not fail to know that this day had gone ill for them ; and a British officer, Lord Orkney, seized the moment to beat a parley. He had only seven battalions and four squadrons with him, but with grand audacity he pointed out the futility of further resistance ; and presently twenty-seven battalions and four squadrons of dismounted dragoons laid down their arms. Among them were some of the finest regiments in the French Army ; and many had not even fired a shot. It was a most cruel fate for brave men.

Borrowing a pencil and a leaf from a Commissary's notebook, Marlborough scrawled a brief note to his wife, not to the Queen, giving her the great news in small compass :

' August 13, 1704. I have not time to say more but to beg you will give my duty to the Queen and let her know her army has had a glorious victory. Monsr. Tallard and two other generals are in my coach and I am following the rest. The bearer, my aide-de-camp, Colonel Parke, will give her an account of what has passed. I shall doe it in a day or two by another more at large.'

So Colonel Parke—he was a Virginian—galloped away and in ten days reached Windsor.

The Queen was sitting in a bay, now part of the Royal Library, on the north side of the Castle, overlooking Eton and the valley of the Thames ; and there Sarah sought her out with her fateful scrap of paper. The room is still called Queen Anne's Closet, and there year after year is placed the old flag of France which is still presented each 13th day of August by the Duke of Marlborough as his feudal rent for the Blenheim Estate. On the walls hang portraits of Marlborough and Parke, a facsimile of the famous note, and a contemporary broadside giving particulars of the troops engaged and of the trophies captured, with a fancy picture of Marlborough with the shell bursting close to his horse. A bust of Queen Anne presides over the whole. Thus in the most august of the Royal palaces is the memory of the great day still kept alive.

IX

FOR it was a great day, a most momentous day, which decided, among other things, that the empire of the new world, apart from the Spanish possessions, was to belong not to France but to England. It was not only that a French army had been beaten, but that French prestige had been utterly shattered—shattered by superior skill, superior fighting power, above all, superior audacity. No two men except Marlborough and Eugene would have dared to take such risks as were taken at Blenheim ; and yet they were not gamblers but cool calculators. They had initiated a new era in the art of war, the era of seeking for swift decision. Some of Eugene's troops had failed him, or Blenheim might have been a still greater day. ' Had the success of Prince Eugene been equal to his merit,' wrote Marlborough to his wife, ' we should in that day's action have made an end of the war.'

The casualties of the Allies numbered over fourteen thousand killed and wounded, upwards

of two thousand being British. Those of
the enemy were never ascertained, but the
prisoners amounted to fifteen thousand and the
deserters to another three or four thousand, so
that at the least their losses must have exceeded
thirty thousand, to say nothing of one hundred
cannon, including light pieces, and trophies innumerable. The Elector of Bavaria and Marsin
hurried with all speed to Lauingen, where they
crossed the Danube and hastened towards
Ulm. Marlborough, after seventeen hours in
the saddle, allowed himself three hours' sleep,
and then busied himself with arrangements for
the wounded, and with a kindly and sympa-
thetic visit to his French prisoners, winning all
hearts by his courtesy and compassion. Not
until the 19th was he able to resume his march,
having first recalled Louis of Baden from Ingolstadt. Meanwhile the defeated armies hastened
back towards the Rhine, rather in flight than retreat, harried daily and hourly by the Imperial
hussars, who hung about their skirts, cutting
off every straggler and bringing back many
prisoners and deserters. The sufferings of the
fugitives were terrible. They had with them
seven thousand unfortunate wounded men, and
the churchyards on their line of march were
choked with their graves as they died. Villeroi

presently came down to meet them, forming
their rearguard from the 24th onward, and on
the 31st the whole of them crossed the Rhine
at Kehl. The Allies began their passage of the
river higher up on the 6th of September ; and
Marlborough closed his campaign in October
and November by recovering Landen, Trèves,
Trarbach and Consaarbrück, thus securing his
winter-quarters on the Moselle in readiness for
next year's operations.

But he was obliged to entrust much of
this latter work to subordinates, being himself
needed elsewhere. Things in the Mediterranean had not gone altogether ill. Gibraltar
had been captured, and the French fleet, after
an indecisive action before Malaga, had retired
to Toulon, from which it ventured not to issue
again during the war. But a detachment of
Allied troops sent to Portugal had accomplished
very little ; and the Duke of Savoy, after turning against France, had found it hard to hold
his own. More troops were required for the
next campaign, and Prussia was the only member of the Grand Alliance that could furnish
them. So Marlborough, the man who could
accomplish everything, travelled from the
Moselle to Berlin, where his adroitness, grace
and tact soon obtained the objects of his

mission. Not until Christmas Day, 1704, was he able to return home, where, disembarking at London Bridge, he found a worthy reception. Parliament voted him its thanks, which Marlborough answered by ascribing his success to his officers and men. The trophies of the victory were carried in triumphant procession to Westminster Hall ; and a few of the flag-staves (for the silk has long since perished) are still to be seen in the chapel of Chelsea Hospital. An Act was passed to convey to him the Manor of Woodstock upon the tenure of presenting a flag bearing the arms of Royal France on the anniversary of the great victory. The Queen further gave orders for the construction of a palace at the royal cost, to be called the Castle of Blenheim. The nation did not grudge Marlborough reward for his great service.

X

MEANWHILE, faction was ever busy in England. Marlborough before starting on his campaign had secured the appointment of two friends, Robert Harley as Secretary of State, and Henry St. John as Secretary at War. But this selection excited extreme discontent among the Whig leaders, and chiefly in Marlborough's son-in-law, Lord Sunderland, who was only conciliated by his nomination to be Ambassador at Vienna. These and other matters being settled, Marlborough in April 1705 repaired to the Hague, intent upon his great plan of advance upon Paris by the Moselle. But the Dutch, who had approved the plan, now rejected it, and it cost him three weeks of negotiation to persuade them again to accept it. The Imperial authorities were slack and irresolute. Louis of Baden, furiously jealous over his absence from Blenheim, thrust every possible obstacle in the way. On the 26th of May Marlborough joined his army at Trèves, but not a man nor a horse of the Imperial contingent appeared. And meanwhile Marshal Villeroi, by moving out against the fortresses on the Meuse, had frightened the Dutch out of their lives. They cried out for Marlborough to return ; and, seeing that nothing could be done on the Moselle, he returned accordingly. He had not approached to within forty miles of Villeroi when the Marshal took the alarm and retired within his fortified lines. These, an anticipation of the continuous trenches of the late German war, ran in a curve from Antwerp in the north-west to Namur in the south-west over a total distance of between seventy and eighty miles. They had taken three years to construct, and would have been formidable enough had the French possessed troops enough to man the whole length of them, and transport enough to keep the men fed. But since they could produce neither the one nor the other, it was not difficult for a skilful general to make a feint against one point so that some other might be weakly guarded, and then to attack the weakened area. Marlborough early broached the project of assailing these lines and obtained the consent of the Dutch Government to attempt it ; but the Dutch generals opposed it, one Schlangenberg being the most vehement among them ; and, though they were overruled, it was certain that they would not work cordially towards execution. With full appreciation of these facts Marlborough laid his plans.

The spot which he had chosen for the attack lay about twenty miles north of Namur. Marlborough directed the Dutch under General Overkirk, a good and loyal soldier, to make a formidable demonstration ten miles to south of this spot ; and Villeroi, falling into the trap, at once assembled forty thousand men to oppose Overkirk. Marlborough then drew together from various points a detachment of about eight thousand men at a point in rear of Overkirk from which he might with equal probability, according to the accepted rules of war, strike in any one of three directions. No man better understood than Marlborough the art of bewildering his enemies. The detachment was most carefully composed. The various units knew nothing of each other, and nothing of the work before them. Moreover, lest the sight of fascines should suggest the storming of entrenchments, the cavalry received orders at the last moment that every trooper should carry an innocent truss of forage on the saddle before him.

On the evening of the 18th of July the heavy baggage of the army started eastward towards

83

Liège. Before nightfall Overkirk, at Marlborough's request, sent a strong body of horse
southward towards Namur. At nightfall the
special detachment fell in silently, and at 9 p.m.
moved off in two columns upon the two selected
points, Neerhespen and Wanghe Castle, about
two miles apart, and both of them about fifteen
miles to north-west. The main body of the
army followed at 10 p.m., and Overkirk had
orders for his van to move in rear of it at 11
p.m. The night was dry, but so dark that the
guides were frequently at fault, and only kept
themselves right by following the trusses dropped
by the advanced party. At 4 a.m. the detachment reached the battlefield of Landen, on the
anniversary of the battle, and halted within a
mile of the Little Geete, one of the most formidable features of the French lines in that section,
and therefore, as Marlborough conjectured,
less likely to be well guarded. It was broad
daylight when they advanced again, but their
movements were concealed by a thick mist
rising from the stream. The first movement
was made upon the bridge of Wanghe, which
was promptly captured by surprise; and the
pontoniers came forward to lay their bridges.
But the infantry, breaking their ranks, dashed
into the water and, scrambling through it

somehow, were soon masters of the Castle. The noise of the firing alarmed two other French posts a little way further up stream, towards which other parties of the Allies were advancing; and seeing red-coats, the garrisons, one of them consisting of three regiments of dragoons, simply took to their heels. Another bridge was thus gained, and with the laying of the pontoons the cavalry began to file across the lines.

The alarm does not appear to have reached the nearest troops of Villeroi's army until 6 o'clock, when they at once turned out with forty squadrons, twenty battalions and a battery of eight triple-barrelled cannon—these last the very latest masterpiece of French military invention. They advanced rapidly, the cavalry leading, until checked by a hollow road, in places very deep, which ran between them and the Allies. Short of this road they halted ; and Marlborough, who had come up with the advanced guard, now assumed personal command. Taking in the situation at a glance, he first occupied the hollow road with infantry, compelling the enemy to fall back, and then forming his thirty-eight squadrons in two lines, the first of them entirely British, he led them across the hollow way to the charge, sword in hand. The enemy, after firing a feeble volley

85

from the saddle, broke in confusion, but being reinforced, rallied and broke the British in their turn. Marlborough, who was riding on the flank, was cut off and left in isolation with his trumpeter. A Bavarian officer galloped at him to cut him down, aiming so furious a blow that he overbalanced himself, fell from his horse, and was captured by the trumpeter. The Allied squadrons rallying then charged again, broke the French past all re-forming, and captured all their guns. The pursuit was checked by the steady bearing of two brigades of French foot, which retired in a hollow square ; and Marlborough knew better than to hurl his horse against unbroken infantry. He sent urgent messages to hasten his own foot, but by some mistake they had been halted after passing the Geete, and it was not until later that his battalions came up at extraordinary speed, the men so fresh and lively that no one would have dreamed that they had been already for twelve hours afoot. Marlborough was anxious to follow up his success forthwith, but the Dutch generals objected, and he was obliged to yield. The loss of the French in this affair seems to have been about two thousand, half of them prisoners, including five general officers, nine field officers, and sixty-five more officers of various grades.

The casualties of the Allies did not exceed two hundred.

' My dearest soul,' wrote Marlborough to his wife, ' my heart is so full of joy for this success that should I write more I should say many follies.' . . . ' The kindness of the troops had transported me,' he explained in a later letter. ' I had none in this action but such as were with me last year . . . which gave occasion to the troops with me to make me very kind expressions even in the heat of the action which I own to you gives me great pleasure and makes me to resolve to endure anything for their sakes.'

In truth the contingents, other than the Dutch, which composed Marlborough's army seem to have guessed very truly at the actual state of affairs. The Dutch, in the words of Marlborough's chaplain, had been bubbled into passing the French lines. Their generals had pronounced them impregnable, and they found themselves safely across them before they knew where they were. As a natural consequence they were furious ; and the non-Dutch elements of the army wished to show Marlborough that they had no sympathy with their surly comrades. Villeroi had retreated hastily upon Louvain, but Marlborough, marching on the

chord of the arc while Villeroi followed the
curve, could have reached it before him ; and
the troops, with the exception of the Dutch,
were willing to second him for all their weari-
ness. But the Dutch hung back. Their generals
considered themselves insulted and meant to
have their revenge.

Advancing next day upon Louvain, the Allies
struck against the rear of the retreating French
columns and captured fifteen hundred prisoners.
But Villeroi having crossed the Dyle extended
his force on a wide front behind it ; and, as it
chanced, heavy rain made the river for some
days impassable. Then Marlborough laid his
plans—much the same in principle as he had
employed for piercing the lines—for forcing the
passage ; but the Dutch deputies were only
after much trouble and delay persuaded to
accept them. On the 29th of July the operations
were begun, and the passage of the river had
actually been secured when the Dutch suddenly
halted their main body for no reason whatever.
Marlborough rode up to ask the cause.
Schlangenberg took him aside and made violent
expostulation, and while the Duke's back was
turned, the Dutch recalled one of their detachments which had crossed the river, and wrecked
the entire operation.

88

With miraculous patience Marlborough re-
frained from complaint, and being unable to
pass the Dyle he turned its head-waters at
Genappe, and wheeling northward approached
the ground now known as the field of Waterloo.
His movements were hastened by the news that
French reinforcements were on their way to
Villeroi from Alsace, where another sulky rival,
Prince Louis of Baden, had by culpable in-
activity failed to detain them. Villeroi on hearing of Marlborough's movement at once shifted
his position to the south bank of the river Yssche.
There, on the 19th of August, Marlborough
made all his dispositions to assail him in front
and flank. Overkirk had already consented
to the plan, but at the last moment the Dutch
deputies interposed. Schlangenberg backed
them with every mark of insolence, and between
them they contrived to fritter away the time
until it was too late to attack. Villeroi, having
received his reinforcements, became decidedly
superior in numbers ; and nothing more could
be done than to level that part of the French
lines.

XI

THUS for a third time a brilliant campaign was
ruined by the treachery and imbecility of the
Dutch. Marlborough had already announced
privately his intention to resign his command
after the shameful behaviour of the Imperial
authorities towards him on the Moselle. He
was now more than ever disgusted, and fortu-
nately he did not stand alone. Public indigna-
tion rose so high both in the United Provinces
and in England that it could not be ignored.
Schlangenberg was disgraced, and the Dutch
Government undertook to appoint deputies
who would take their orders from Marlborough
instead of giving them to him. ' I wish we
may find the effects of them,' was the Duke's
dry comment. Nevertheless he did not resign
his command. Louis XIV., as he knew, had
in August secretly proposed to the Dutch
Government a treaty of peace highly advan-
tageous to the United Provinces ; and it was
therefore of the utmost importance to avoid
any dispute that might weaken the Grand

Alliance. Without hesitation he sacrificed his private feelings to the common good. During his absence, as an eye-witness said, the army was a body without a soul.

Wearied out by the fatigue and disappointments of the past months, Marlborough was suffering greatly in health. 'I am worn to nothing,' he wrote at this time ; 'I am so extremely lean that it is uneasy to me when I am in bed.' None the less the exigencies of the Grand Alliance compelled him in October to make the long journey to Vienna in order to keep the Imperial Court up to the mark, to advise as to the next campaign, and to arrange for raising the necessary funds in England. He fulfilled his mission with an address and courage which made the Emperor and all of his ministers most friendly. The Emperor conferred upon him the principality of Mindelheim ; and at the end of November Marlborough left Vienna for Berlin. There he found the King of Prussia greatly and excusably incensed against both the Emperor and the Dutch. With his usual charm and adroitness he contrived to soothe him and to obtain a renewal of the treaty for the furnishing of a Prussian contingent. From Berlin he passed on to Hanover, where he had to smooth the plumes of the old Electress Sophia, which had been sadly ruffled by the vagaries of the factions in the English Parliament. From Hanover he journeyed to the Hague, where he had much trouble in arranging for a Dutch loan to the Emperor ; and not until January 1706 could he return to England. There politicians and people were justifiably discontented with the issue of the last campaign, and the usual factions and squabbles were in full play. But what with Eugene's operations in Italy and Allied operations in Spain, over and above operations in Flanders, the Duke could spare little attention for the petty intrigues of English political circles. His diplomatic duties were more than sufficient for one man, quite apart from all military occupations.

His own wish was to conduct his next campaign in company with Eugene in Italy, having resolved to have nothing more to do either with Imperialists in the East nor, if possible, with the Dutch in the North. He had almost persuaded the Dutch to agree to this arrangement, when his plans were upset by one of his old tormentors. Prince Louis of Baden had allowed himself to be surprised and roughly handled by Villars on the Rhine ; and the Dutch, yielding to their wonted timidity, entreated the Duke to return to Flanders. In April accordingly he went to the Hague, and in May he learned that Villeroi had actually summoned courage to advance eastward from the Dyle. The Marshal, not knowing that he had owed his safety in 1705 to the treachery of the Dutch deputies and generals, had latterly been speaking of Marlborough with a certain patronising contempt. The Duke promptly concentrated sixty thousand men a little south of Maastricht, and marched westward to meet him. At 8 a.m. on Whitsunday, the 23rd of May, Cadogan, who had ridden forward to mark out a camp by the village of Ramillies, dimly descried troops moving in the mist before him, and two hours later could perceive the entire French army in full march. Villeroi had not expected to meet Marlborough until twenty-four hours later—the Duke in fact had a way of presenting himself before his enemies a day earlier than he was looked for—but he had reached a favourable position on the highest ground of the table-land of Brabant, and was content. It was true that the great Luxemburg had rejected this same position as faulty, but Villeroi was satisfied with it, and proceeded to deploy for action. This front, slightly concave in form, faced due east. His right, or southern flank

rested on the marshy, sluggish little river
Mehaigne. Four villages stood out like bastions
on his front, Tavières on the Mehaigne on his
right, Ramillies on his right centre, Offus on
his left centre, and Autréglise on his extreme
left. The front from Autréglise to Ramillies—
about three thousand yards—was covered by
the swampy meadows of the Little Geete ;
but from Ramillies to Tavières—about twenty-
five hundred yards—was sound open ground,
sloping gently down to eastward, an ideal field
for cavalry action. Here therefore Villeroi
drew up seventy-eight squadrons, including the
famous French household cavalry (*Maison du
Roi*) in three lines. He occupied all the villages
with infantry, and drew up the rest of his foot
in two lines between Ramillies and Autréglise,
with fifty more squadrons in third line behind
them. Villeroi had in all sixty-two thousand
men, and was confident of success.

Marlborough speedily made up his mind to
break the French right on the open ground
between Tavières and Ramillies, and accordingly he directed the whole of the British troops
against Villeroi's left. Now Villeroi had orders
from his King to give particular attention to
that part of the line which should bear the first
shock of the English troops ; and, seeing the

red-coats in full stride towards his left, he withdrew troops from his centre and right to reinforce that point. At about 1.30 p.m. the
artillery opened fire on both sides, and at about
3 p.m. the British began their advance over the
swamp between Offus and Autréglise. Their
leader, Lord Orkney, had orders to make only
a feint attack. The swamp, owing to recent
heavy rain, was supposed to be impassable,
but the British infantry managed to cross it,
and even a few squadrons of British cavalry,
taught by the lesson of the Nebel at Blenheim,
struggled over it, to cover their right flank.
Messenger after messenger galloped to Orkney
to bid him stop, but he, imagining that his
orders had been due to a misconception of the
state of the ground, continued to press on. At
last, after ten aides-de-camp in succession had
remonstrated with him in vain, Cadogan came
to him in person, and told him that, if he made
his attack prematurely, there was no possibility
of supporting him. Thereupon very reluctantly
Orkney gave the word for his twelve battalions
to retire, sheltering the movement with the
First Guards and the Royal Scots. The cavalry
then withdrew into a dip of the ground, out of
sight of the French, followed by the second line
of infantry, while the first line of infantry halted

95

upon the slope in full view of the enemy. Then, always concealed from the French, the second line together with eighteen squadrons of foreign horse filed away towards the French right. Some of Villeroi's officers suspected this movement, but he would not listen to them. The red-coats had proved that the ground before his left could be traversed, both by foot and horse ; and nothing would induce him to weaken himself in that quarter.

Then the attack began in earnest. Four Dutch battalions with two guns marched out against Tavières with forty-eight Dutch squadrons, backed by twenty-one Danish squadrons, moving in accordance with them. The infantry stormed into Tavières without hesitation, driving the French infantry out headlong, whereupon the commander of the French cavalry dismounted fourteen squadrons of dragoons of his third line and sent the men, together with two Swiss battalions, to recover the village. They were checked by a crushing fire from the Dutch infantry ; and Overkirk seized the moment to launch his twenty-one squadrons upon them. The Danes charged home. The Swiss and dragoons were trampled out of existence. The horses of the dismounted dragoons bolted, and thus fourteen

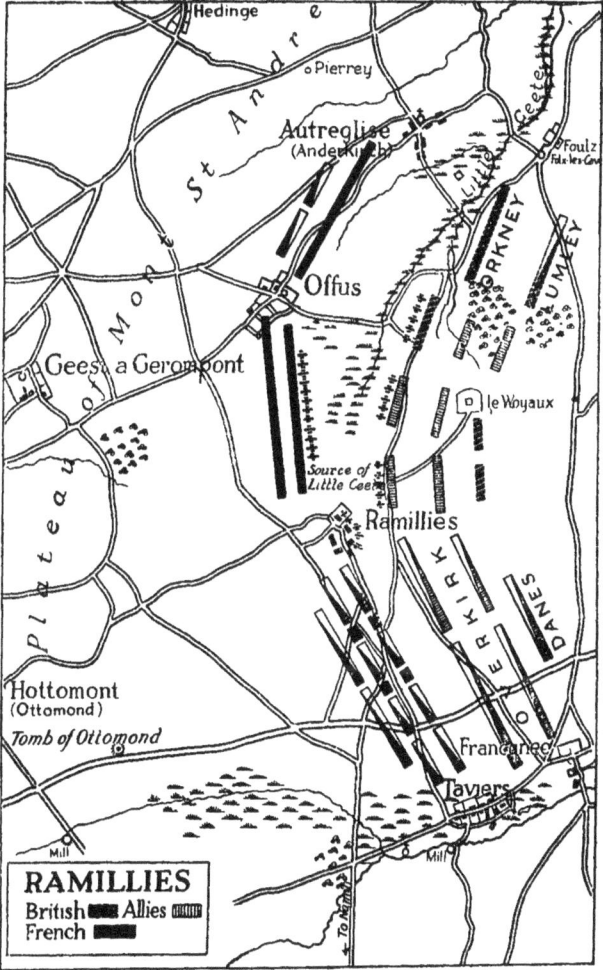

Hedinge
o Pierrey
st André
Autreglise
(Anderkirch)
Foulz
Fox-les-Cave
ORKNEY
UMKEY
Offus
Geest a Gerompont
le Woyaux
Plateau of Mont
Source of
Little Geet
Ramillies
ERKIRK
DANES
Hottomont
(Ottomond)
Tomb of Ottomond
Franquenec
Taviers
Mill
Mill
To Mill

RAMILLIES
British ▰▰▰ Allies ▥▥▥
French ▰▰▰

G

French squadrons were put out of action at a stroke.

Then Overkirk gathered his forty-eight squadrons together for attack upon the sixty-four that still remained of the French ; and simultaneously Marlborough hurled twelve battalions against Ramillies, thus diverting every French gun to fire towards that village. Overkirk charged, not without success at certain points; but the odds against him were great, and for the most part he was overborne. Marlborough then sent urgent orders to his right for every squadron, except the British, to join him forthwith, and meanwhile in person he led the eighteen squadrons which he had recalled from his own right into action. In the *mêlée* which followed he was recognised and assailed, but was able to fight his way out until his horse came down at a ditch and threw him. He was ridden over, but not seriously hurt, and regaining his feet ran to take refuge with the infantry that was engaged before Ramillies. A British officer in command of foreign troops threw out a couple of battalions to rescue him, and,though the Duke's pursuers rode actually on to the bayonets in their eagerness, he was saved. His aide-de-camp dismounting gave him his own horse, and his equerry, Colonel Bingfield, held the stirrup for him. Before he was well in the saddle, the hand suddenly dropped the stirrup and the body of Bingfield fell to the ground, his head having been carried away by a cannon-shot.

Then the cavalry summoned from the Allied right came galloping up, but the contest had already been decided by the squadrons under Marlborough's own command. The Dutch had rallied and renewed the fight. The Danes had likewise rallied and, led with great skill, had fallen upon the right flank of the French. Part of the French second line of horse fled away. Those that stood to meet the charge were pressed into the marshes of the Little Geete.

The French right, between Tavières and Ramillies, was absolutely broken ; the Allied horse was pouring into the gap, and the beaten French horse were streaming headlong along the rear of their army. Villeroi, calling forward the cavalry of his left, tried to form a new front for his right wing ; but the ground was en-cumbered by his baggage train, and the attempt failed. Meanwhile Ramillies had been carried after the repulse of two assaults ; and the troops that had mastered it turned upon the right flank of the French array. Marlborough then ordered his whole line to advance. The British, without

99

awaiting the word, dashed forward upon Autréglise ; and the whole of Villeroi's centre and left, with the exception of a few brave battalions between Ramillies and Offus, gave way and fell back. They retired at first in fair order, but the British cavalry coming up rode down in one quarter the rearguard of Bavarian horse and in another two French battalions of the King's regiment. Then the retreat became a rout. The narrow ways were blocked by broken-down waggons and abandoned guns, and the crush of the fugitives was appalling. The pursuit began soon after 6 p.m., and was carried on relentlessly by the British far into the night. Not until 2 a.m. did the cavalry pause, having then reached Meldert, twelve miles from the battlefield. Orkney with some few squadrons actually spurred on to Louvain itself, ten miles beyond Meldert, and rekindling the panic sent the French flying beyond the Dyle. Marlborough himself, battered and bruised though he was, reached Meldert at midnight after twenty-eight hours in the saddle, allowed himself three hours' sleep, and started off again just as the first of his infantry, with marvellous spirit, came tramping in. Still he pushed on westward, with the French flying before him, until the 27th, when he at last granted his weary troops a halt. But it was not for long. Villeroi had retired to his lines about Ghent ; but Marlborough, sending forward a detachment to bridge the Scheldt below Oudenarde, threatened to cut off his retreat to France and forced him to retire up the Lys to Courtrai. Strong places in the Spanish Netherlands surrendered in rapid succession—Louvain, Brussels, Malines, Lierre, Alost, Ghent, Bruges, Damme, Oudenarde and Antwerp—and thus within a fortnight of the victory the whole of Flanders and Brabant, with the exception of a few minor fortresses, had succumbed to the Allies, and the French had been driven within their own boundaries.

It was a great, a stupendous success, and gained at no great cost. The casualties of the Allies, which fell chiefly on the Dutch and Danes, numbered from four to five thousand. Those of the French amounted to thirteen thousand killed, wounded and prisoners, besides at least two thousand deserters. They lost all their guns and baggage, besides trophies without number, and, though comparatively few had been engaged, the whole were utterly beaten and demoralised. Marlborough reported his victory to the Queen, but it was to his wife that he poured out his soul :

'Monday, May 24th, 11 o'clock. I did not tell my dearest soul in my last the design I had of engaging the enemy if possible to a battle, fearing the concern she had for me might make her uneasy ; but I can now give her the satis-faction of letting her know that on Sunday last we fought, and that God Almighty has been pleased to give us a victory. I must leave the particulars to this bearer, Colonel Richards, for having been on horseback all Sunday and after the battle marching all night, my head aches to that degree that it is very uneasy to me to write. Poor Bingfield holding my stirrup for me and helping me on horseback was killed. I am told that he leaves his wife and mother in poor condition. I can't write to any of my children, so that you will let them know I am well, and that I desire they will thank God for preserving me. And pray give my duty to the Queen and let her know the truth of my heart that the greatest pleasure I have in this success is that it may be a great service to her affairs, for I am very sensible of her goodness to me and mine. Pray believe me when I assure you that I love you more than I can express.'

Bruised and shaken by a bad fall from his horse, worn out by the strenuous work of the battle and the still more exhausting toil of the pursuit, with a thousand things to think of and a hundred orders to be given, and with a blinding headache as the result of all these things, the greatest man in Europe could still think above all of the woman whom he loved best in the world, sparing her all anxiety and assuring her that in his heart she came before everybody and everything. The letter written on Monday reached Sarah on Thursday night ; and on Friday she went to condole with the widowed Mrs. Bingfield, and to tell her that the Queen had granted her a pension for life. What reward Colonel Richards may have received we know not ; but he lives in history as the commander of the garrison of Alicante, who in 1709 refused to surrender the fort, which had been undermined by the French, and was swallowed up quick with eighty of his men when the mine was exploded. Thus does one hero make many.

XII

KING LOUIS XIV. now summoned Villars with
the greater part of his army from the Rhine to
the Lys, and, through the criminal apathy and
neglect of Prince Louis of Baden, he was
allowed to do so unhindered. Other French
troops were brought back from Italy, and Villeroi was superseded by Vendôme ; but all alike
looked on helplessly while Marlborough besieged and captured in succession Ostend,
Menin, Dendermonde and Ath. In October
heavy rain put a stop to further operations and
closed the marvellous campaign of Ramillies.

Its immediate result was very nearly to dissolve the Grand Alliance. The Spanish Netherlands had been recovered, and the question
arose as to who should occupy and govern them.
The Emperor claimed them and wished to
instal Marlborough as Governor with £60,000
a year. Marlborough at once wrote privately
to the Dutch Government that he would not
accept the appointment without their approval;
but the Dutch were furious. They wanted the

Spanish Netherlands for themselves, and Louis
XIV. adroitly egged them on by offering them
a separate peace and a new partition of the
Spanish Empire. The offer was neutralised
by most brilliant operations of Eugene in Italy,
which laid the Milanese within the grasp of
the Emperor. He, however, was naturally also
furious at the pretensions of the Dutch; and
there was the further complication that the
people of the Spanish Netherlands abominated all Dutchmen. Altogether there was a
very pretty quarrel, which gave Marlborough
untold anxiety and was never really composed.
England, under his guidance, was working for
the common cause, but she worked alone.
Every other member of the Alliance was working for herself. The views of the Dutch and
Austrians as to the barrier which should be
erected in the Spanish Netherlands against
French aggression were utterly irreconcilable;
and Marlborough, as the friend of each party,
naturally incurred the suspicion and dislike of
both.

He had a great reception when he returned
to England at the end of November, but he
found what is called a political crisis disturb-
ing the Government. It was of the usual kind.
The Whigs, who had a majority in Parliament,

naturally claimed a larger share of place and
power, and by skilful manœuvring were in a
position to exact it. The Queen was not dis-
posed to give way to them ; yet on Marlborough's persuasion consented to conciliate
them by appointing Sunderland to be Secretary
of State. But by so doing Marlborough alien-
ated the Queen. Then, as usual, he was called
upon to resolve a new foreign complication.
The French were intriguing with the Court of
Sweden, and the young King Charles XII., as it
chanced, had taken offence over some petty
differences with the Emperor. Since, before
he was twenty-one, he had smashed the armies
of the three Powers which designed to partition
his kingdom and was even at the moment
occupying the territory of one of them, his
junction with the French might be formidable.
The Continental Allies were seriously alarmed,
and of course in their trouble came to Marlborough. So in April 1707 he hurried away to
Saxony, saw Charles there, and by flattery,
gross but not too gross for the King of Sweden,
secured him to benevolence towards the Grand
Alliance. He returned by way of Berlin, and
by the first week in May had reached the Hague.

His project for the new campaign assigned
only a subordinate part to himself. The Spanish

Netherlands had been recovered. The Milanese and Naples lay at the Emperor's mercy. The last campaign in Spain had gone fairly well for the Imperialists. A heavy blow in the Mediterranean should suffice to bring France to terms. He designed, therefore, that the Imperial troops under Eugene should invade Provence by way of Savoy, supported at sea by the navies of the Maritime Powers, and that the operations should culminate in the siege and capture of Toulon, which would be a crushing blow to France. Since the Austrians had declined to advance on Paris by way of the Moselle, and the Allies were consequently entangled among the fortresses of Northern France, he thought this stroke, coupled with vigorous action in Spain, the most likely to bring the war to an end.

On reaching the Hague, Marlborough was at once met by bad news. The French victory at Almansa had upset all the good done in Spain. This was followed by a series of mistakes and miscarriages. The Margrave of Baireuth, who had succeeded Louis of Baden, deceased, upon the Rhine, allowed himself to be surprised and discomfited by Villars. The Austrians frittered away their time and their men by invading Naples instead of Provence, which enabled Vendôme for long to confront Marlborough in the Low Countries with greatly superior forces. Then, when the Austrians finally advanced upon Toulon, they did so half-heartedly and in insufficient strength. They did indeed draw some French troops from Flanders and enable Marlborough to move. But the Dutch deputies were careful to intervene upon the one occasion when he could have struck a blow ; and incessant rain practically forbade operations for weeks on either side. Thus the campaign of 1707 came to naught ; and it was only by continual exertion that Marlborough could hold the Grand Alliance together.

XIII

RETURNING home in November, the Duke was
confronted with difficulties not less trying than
at the front. There were dissensions in the
Cabinet. Sarah by her domineering ways had
offended the Queen, and thrown her into the
arms of another lady of her household, Abigail
Masham, a clever woman who managed Anne
with tact. The general outcome of a series of
political incidents too complicated for narration
here was that Harley was dismissed from office,
that St. John resigned, and that two able men
upon whom Marlborough had counted as
friends were converted into enemies. At the
root of the whole matter was Whig greed for
office, without any regard to the efficient conduct of the war. The spring of 1708 was wasted
by a futile endeavour of the French King to set
the Pretender afoot in Scotland with a French
force at his back, an enterprise which was easily
foiled by Marlborough's naval and military dispositions. Early in April Marlborough crossed
to the Hague, where he met Prince Eugene ;

and it was arranged that the Prince should take charge of an army on the Moselle, nominally for operations in that quarter, but really to march and join Marlborough as soon as possible, and with him to force the French to action. Meanwhile the French by great efforts had collected one hundred thousand men for the war in Flanders, under the nominal command of the heir to the French throne, with Vendôme under him. Marlborough had as yet no more than eighty thousand. In May the French advanced in superior numbers, and after some preliminary manœuvres struck westward, where they received through treachery the surrender of Bruges and Ghent. This misfortune was due entirely to the misgovernment of the Dutch, which promised to alienate every city in the Spanish Netherlands from the Grand Alliance. However, there the matter was. The keys of the Scheldt and Lys were lost to the Allies, and Marlborough, who was suffering from fever, became anxious, for he knew not where this process of surrender might end. Vendôme, to assure himself of the line of the Scheldt, sent a detachment to invest Oudenarde, and moved with his main army on the 9th of July towards Lessines on the Dender, about fourteen miles to south-east of Oudenarde, from which position

he designed to cover the siege. Marlborough
lay at Assche, more than twenty miles as the
crow flies from Lessines, Eugene being with him
though without his army. At 2 a.m. of that
same day, the 9th, Marlborough's army began
its march, and before 11 a.m. covered fifteen
miles. At 4 p.m. Cadogan moved on with a
detachment of about five thousand horse and
foot, and at sunset the whole army followed
them. At midnight an advanced party of
Cadogan's men occupied Lessines. At 4 a.m.
on the 10th the rest of the detachment arrived
and threw bridges over the Dender, and at
11 a.m. the main body marched in and pitched
their camp on the very ground that Vendôme
had chosen for his own troops. They had
traversed thirty miles in thirty-three hours.

Once again Marlborough had arrived a day
earlier than he was expected, and had moreover interposed himself between the French
army and the French frontier. Vendôme
turned north-westward to shelter himself behind
the Scheldt and to bar the access of the Allies
to Bruges ; but Marlborough was not going to
let him off so easily. At 1 a.m. on the 11th
Cadogan started off with sixteen battalions
(four of them British) and thirty squadrons—
say ten thousand men in all—and reaching

the Scheldt about a mile below Oudenarde began to throw bridges across the river. The French vanguard had already crossed the stream at Gavre, about ten miles below Oudenarde, but the main body was still on the same bank—the eastern—with Cadogan's detachment, and serenely unconscious that any enemy was near. Some of Cadogan's cavalry surprised the foragers of the French vanguard on the opposite bank and took a few prisoners, but other French troopers carried the news to Biron, who commanded the French vanguard ; and he appears to have mistaken Cadogan's detachment for the entire Allied army. There was some excuse for the mistake, for, on hearing from Cadogan that the French had not yet passed the Scheldt, Marlborough had ordered half of his horse to advance rapidly to his support, and the column could be seen trotting south-westward. Vendôme, however, treated the whole report with incredulity. His main body continued to defile across the river at Gavre, and not until 1 p.m. or later did he realise that he must fight. It was open to him to meet the Allies either on the flat ground alongside the river or on a line of heights about a mile beyond it. He seems to have decided that the former would be the better course ;

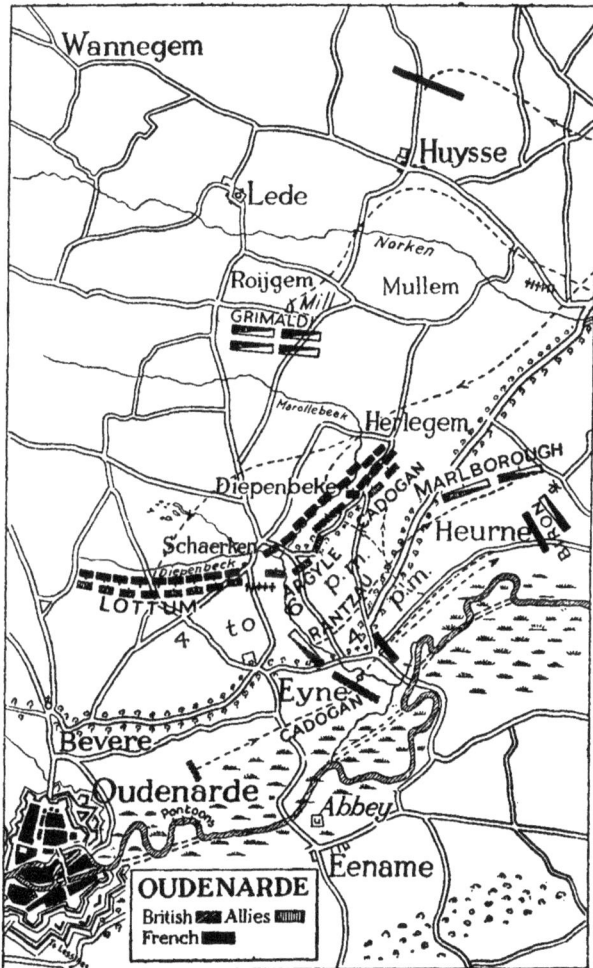

OUDENARDE
British ▨ Allies ▥
French ▬

H

and accordingly four battalions were thrown into the village of Eyne, rather more than a mile below Oudenarde, and three more, with a dozen squadrons, into Heurne, another village a mile below Eyne. Meanwhile Marlborough, taking all risks, passed half of his cavalry across the river at Oudenarde, ranged them beyond the town and could only wait impatiently for his infantry.

They began to come up before 3 p.m., and now it was observed that the French main army was taking up its position on the heights beyond the Scheldt, leaving the garrisons of Eyne and Heurne in isolation. Cadogan launched his British brigade at Eyne and made short work of it. Three of the four battalions in the village laid down their arms after a short encounter, and the fourth, while trying to withdraw to Heurne, was overtaken by some squadrons of Hanoverian dragoons and destroyed. The three battalions in Heurne, which were advancing to the support of their comrades, thereupon fled in panic to the position of their main army, and their supporting cavalry were preparing to move in the same direction when they were charged by the Hanoverians and utterly dispersed. In their flight they crashed into the flank of the rearguard of their main army, which was just

114

coming into position, and the pursuing Hanoverians caused much confusion before they were
driven off. The Electoral Prince of Hanover,
later King George II., rode with the Hanoverians in this charge, and was conspicuous for
his valour.

This was a good beginning to a general
action, but few of Marlborough's battalions
had yet come up, whereas Vendôme's entire
host was on the spot if he should choose to
counter-attack upon Marlborough's left. Marlborough, alive to the danger, pushed the fourteen battalions which he had in hand half a
mile forward towards the French position, resting their flanks upon two villages, and posting
his cavalry on either flank of these villages.
About 5 p.m. thirty French battalions debouched
against this line, but the ground was strongly
enclosed, and the Allies, fighting fiercely, held
their own until gradually reinforced by the
arrival of the main army. Marlborough now
handed over command of his right wing to
Eugene, and himself took command of the left.
Eugene was at one moment hard pressed, but,
as battalion after battalion came up, was able
to recover lost ground. On the left the French
fought with great steadiness and gallantry, but
were gradually pushed back. Their right flank,

as Marlborough had noted, was in the air, and he now ordered Overkirk and his cavalry which stood above Oudenarde to wheel to the right and extend his horse round the flank and rear of the French right wing. The gallant old man obeyed with alacrity, bearing down the French cavalry before him. The infantry of the Allied left wing pushed forward and began steadily to envelop the French right wing. Vendôme tried to avert disaster by bringing up troops from his centre and left, but they only added to the congestion and confusion. At last about 9 p.m. the circle of the Allies had closed in so straitly upon the French right wing that Marlborough, fearful lest his men should engage each other in the darkness, gave the order to cease fire. Great numbers of the French then contrived to escape, but presently all the drums of the Allies began to beat the French call for retreat, while the Huguenot officers shouted '*À moi Picardie ! À moi Roussillon !*' to gather the fragments of the French regiments about them. Thus some thousands of prisoners were gleaned, though nothing to the harvest which would have been reaped by another hour of daylight. Utter confusion reigned in the French host, and though Vendôme tried in vain to keep it together until

morning, the whole ran off in disorder towards Ghent. Their losses amounted to fifteen
thousand, including nine thousand prisoners.
Marlborough declared that with two hours
more of daylight he would have ended the
war.

The action of Oudenarde was remarkable at
that period since it presented a general engagement without any formal order of battle. Beyond doubt Marlborough took great risks, but
a victory was all-important at that moment to
redeem an unfavourable situation. His great
stroke was the wonderful march that thrust
his army between Vendôme's and the French
frontier. No one except himself and possibly
Eugene would have dared to attempt it. It
was in itself such a surprise that it made the
work of the actual battle, though hazardous,
comparatively simple. But only a commander
who could count upon his troops for extraordinary exertions could have relied upon
such an effort. Such was the magic of Marlborough's leadership that every soldier in his
army took the surrender of Bruges and Ghent
as a personal affront and burned to avenge it.
And they did so by marching fifty miles, including the passage of two broad rivers, between 2 a.m. on Monday and 2 p.m. on

Wednesday, at which latter hour they went not into camp but into action.

Marlborough gave his force two days' halt after the battle, and Vendôme made haste to secure himself behind the Bruges-Ghent Canal. The French army of the Moselle under the Duke of Berwick, hurrying to his aid, took post at Douai. Eugene's army likewise came up and was stationed at Brussels. Marlborough encamped on French territory between Ypres and Commines, and did all that he could by raids and by levying of contributions to draw Vendôme out of his lines, but in vain. The question arose what should be done next. Marlborough was for advancing upon Abbeville at the mouth of the Somme, there to combine operations with a naval expedition which was ready to start from the Isle of Wight, and making the whole movement safe by masking the fortress of Lille. The project for once seemed too audacious even for Eugene, who was unwilling to undertake it unless Lille were first captured. Marlborough hated sieges, but he deferred to Eugene's opinion and agreed to the siege of Lille. It was a formidable undertaking, for Lille was Vauban's masterpiece, girt about not with a single but with a triple line of fortifications, and the place was strongly

118

garrisoned. Moreover, since the enemy still held the keys of the Scheldt and Lys, it would be necessary to drag the whole of the siege material from Brussels, a distance of seventy-five miles ; and this would require sixteen thousand horses. Vendôme in the north and Berwick at Douai had between them one hundred and ten thousand men, yet so skilfully was the march of the huge unwieldy convoy conducted that its progress was hardly impeded, and not a single waggon was lost. Of all the achievements of Marlborough and Eugene this was esteemed by contemporary military men to be the greatest.

Lille was invested on the 13th of August, Eugene undertaking the work of the siege while Marlborough took charge of the covering army. Vendôme and Berwick presently united their forces, which Marlborough allowed them to do without hindrance, and they entered the plain of Lille with ninety-four thousand men. They had positive orders to risk a battle, which the Allied commanders, though they had but eighty-four thousand men, freely offered them. But after a week's hesitation Vendôme withdrew, having accomplished nothing, though, but for the interposition of the Dutch deputies, he would have had an engagement forced upon him whether he liked it or not. The French then fell back to strong positions on the Scarpe and Scheldt between Douai and Ghent so as to threaten all convoys passing from Brussels. Marlborough, quite prepared for this, opened a new base at Ostend. Vendôme thereupon sent twenty-two thousand men to attack the first convoy coming from Ostend. They were utterly worsted at Wynendal by half their number of the Allies under the English General Webb. Vendôme then advanced towards Ostend with a considerable force, and opening the dykes laid much of the country under water. Marlborough brought this stroke to naught by using high-wheeled vehicles and punts to convey his material. The operations before Lille itself went forward rather slowly, for Marshal Boufflers conducted the defence with not less gallantry than skill. Nevertheless after a leaguer of sixty days the city capitulated on the 1st of October, and Eugene now bent himself to reduce the citadel.

Then in November the Elector of Bavaria came on the scene from the Rhine and laid siege to Brussels with fifteen thousand men. If the Elector of Hanover, the future George I., had not shown unpardonable apathy, the Bavarians should never have been allowed to make this movement, but there the Bavarians were, and it was difficult to see how their blow was to be countered. Spreading reports that he was about to place his troops in winter-quarters, and making sundry feint marches to strengthen those reports, Marlborough on the night of the 26th November suddenly and swiftly moved eastward with the covering army, crossed the Scheldt at two different points before the enemy had an idea that he was near them, and captured a thousand prisoners. Then, sending the bulk of his force back to Lille, he pushed on with a detachment of cavalry and two battalions of English Guards to Alost. There he was still twelve miles distant from Brussels, but he learned on his arrival that the Elector had already raised the siege and hurried away. The fact that Marlborough was coming was quite enough for him.

At length on the 9th of December, Boufflers and his heroic garrison marched out of the citadel of Lille with the honours of war, and within the next fortnight Bruges and Ghent were both of them recovered. Then at last, after a prolonged campaign, the Allied army went into winter-quarters. But even so, Marl-borough had not forgotten naval operations nor the Mediterranean. On the very day when the tidings of the fall of Lille reached London there came also the news that General Stanhope, with a part of the forces set apart for Spain, had captured the island of Minorca.

XIV

THE success of the past campaign prompted Parliament to be liberal in voting supplies for the next. But meanwhile an abnormally severe winter had reduced France to such misery that Louis XIV. offered to make peace at almost any price. An enormous bribe was tendered to Marlborough by the French negotiators in the hope of obtaining from him certain concessions, but he refused even to look at it. Left to himself he would, for the sake of all parties, almost certainly have closed the war upon very favourable terms to England ; but his influence at home was fast waning. The Whigs were pressing insatiably for more power, Sarah had quarrelled bitterly with the Queen over a trifling matter ; and Abigail Masham's voice was steadily gaining power with her royal mistress. Thus Marlborough was compelled by instructions from London to impose conditions which Louis could not possibly accept. Roused by the insult to their nation, the French made extraordinary efforts to recruit their armies, and Villars was summoned from the Rhine to take command in Flanders. He threw up lines of extraordinary strength from the Scarpe at Douai to the Lys, with the object of closing France against invasion, and within these he lay unassailable. Marlborough and Eugene marched against him with one hundred and ten thousand men, and made great demonstrations of attack. Villars, who had but eighty thousand men, promptly summoned the greater part of the garrison of Tournai to join him, whereupon, on the night of the 26th of June, Marlborough quietly marched away eastward, and on the morning of the 27th the army to its great astonishment found itself investing Tournai. The place was immensely strong, but was undermanned ; and, with Marlborough in personal direction of the siege, its fate was certain. On the 19th of July the city surrendered ; and then followed the reduction of the citadel, a very desperate enterprise, for the subterranean works were more numerous and formidable than those above ground. Continual rain greatly hampered the operations, but on the 3rd of September the citadel capitulated.

Before the end of the siege Marlborough and Eugene, leaving a sufficient force behind them, had moved back with the main army before the French lines at Douai. Those lines might be turned, though they could not be forced, and the two commanders had decided that their next enterprise should be the siege of Mons. Accordingly, on the 31st of August, Lord Orkney with twenty squadrons and all the grenadier-companies of the army marched silently and swiftly eastward towards St. Ghislain on the Haine, about six miles west of Mons. Three days later, upon the fall of Tournai, the Prince of Hesse Cassel with sixty squadrons and four thousand foot started in the same direction at 4 p.m. Reaching St. Ghislain he learned from Orkney that the place was too strong to be carried by Orkney's small force, and accordingly he pushed on. Rain was falling in torrents, but none the less he continued his march until at 2 a.m. on the 6th he wheeled south and crossed the Haine at Obourg, three miles to north-east of Mons. There he crossed the ground which was so gallantly held by Smith-Dorrien's 8th Infantry Brigade on 23rd August 1914, passed on to some entrenchments which had been constructed during the last war, and finding them weakly guarded, strode over them at noon unopposed. He had traversed fifty-three miles in fifty-six hours. On the same

evening the main body of the army arrived and
invested Mons on the eastern side.

Villars, as soon as he was sure of the direction
which the Allies had taken, concentrated his
army and moved eastward, with a firm resolution to save Mons. His approach to the fortress
was barred by a broad belt of forest, through
which ran the two Roman roads which, con-
verging from north and north-east, meet at
Bavai, about twelve miles south and west of
Mons, and thence formed the highway to Paris.
There were three ways of traversing this belt.
Villars could skirt it by the north, or he could
pass through it by one of two gaps, the more
northerly called the gap of Boussu, the southerly
called the gap of Malplaquet. The two first
of these were closed by the armies of Eugene
and Marlborough, but the gap of Malplaquet
was open, and this Villars occupied with an
advanced detachment early on the morning
of the 8th. At 8 a.m. Marlborough and Eugene
making a personal reconnaissance discovered
this detachment, and gave orders for their
forces to shift position to southward, at the
same time bringing up artillery to check the
further advance of the French. Villars halted
at the western entrance and began to entrench
himself. Heavy rain prevented Eugene's army

from complete junction with Marlborough's until next day, the 9th, but must also have delayed the arrival of the rear of Villars's columns after a long march. On the 10th Marlborough, observing the rapid progress of Villars' earthworks, proposed to attack at once. Eugene, however, thought that it would be wiser to await the arrival of eighteen battalions which were on their way from Tournai, and Marlborough gave way. Villars meanwhile made the best use of his time. The actual gap he covered with a chain of nine redans, with spaces between them to allow for the passage of cavalry. On his left the forest called the forest of Taisnières ran almost at right angles to this line of redans, and the entrenchments followed its edge for about a thousand yards, then doubled back so as to form a salient angle, and then again ran forwards so as to form a re-entrant. The depth of the wood at this point was about a thousand yards, and on the open plateau in rear of it were two more lines of entrenchments. On his right, called the forest of Laignières, the entrenchments likewise were carried deep into the wood, the right being thrown back from the edge so as to present a salient angle. Villars filled the entrenchments with his infantry, massed his cavalry in two lines upon the open plateau in rear, and with confidence awaited attack.

Marlborough and Eugene quickly realised the strength and weakness of the French position. The entrenchments in the gap itself offered in general a huge re-entrant angle which it would be madness to assail. They determined, therefore, to make feints only against Villars's centre and right, and to throw their main strength against his left, in the forest of Taisnières, directing also a wide turning movement against his left flank. The Dutch infantry under the Prince of Orange—thirty-one battalions—were to make the demonstration against Villars's right and right centre, with twenty-one Dutch squadrons in support. Lord Orkney, with fifteen British battalions and thirty Dutch squadrons, was to threaten the left centre. Sixty-two battalions, Austrian and British, were to deliver the main assault on the entrenchments of Taisnières Forest. General Withers with nineteen battalions and six squadrons was to make the wide turning movement through the forest upon Villars's left flank. The remainder of the cavalry was massed in rear of the centre. The Allied commanders reckoned that Villars must in time weaken his centre to strengthen his left, and decided that at the right moment the feint attack on the centre should be made real, that the French centre should be pierced, and the French army broken up.

The morning of the 11th broke with heavy mist, under cover of which forty guns were brought into position opposite to the entrenchments of Taisnières Forest. The chaplains read prayers at the head of each regiment ; and at 9 a.m. the columns of attack were launched against those same entrenchments. The first assault was repulsed with heavy loss at all points. The second fared at first little better, and Villars was on the point of making a counter-attack when Marlborough in person threatened his flank with thirty squadrons and compelled him quickly to withdraw his battalions. By a desperate effort the Allies mastered the defences at one point, and the French resistance sensibly weakened. Gradually the French left wing was forced back into the wood, and there was savage fighting among the trees. All order was lost ; but the turning movement of Withers was beginning to make itself felt, and the Allies steadily gained ground. Villars, as Marlborough and Eugene had anticipated, had been obliged to weaken his centre in order to reinforce his left ; but unfortunately the Dutch were in no condition to take advantage of it. With criminal folly the Prince of Orange, instead of confining himself to demonstration, had led his battalions right into the heart of the re-entrant angle, and though they had striven most gallantly to accomplish the impossible, they had been beaten back with terrible losses. Six thousand of the best of the Dutch infantry had fallen, and the whole of Marlborough's centre at the crisis of the battle was in confusion. It was not the first nor was it to be the last occasion that a royal prince had brought about disaster by trying to pose as a great commander. Marlborough and Eugene were fully occupied for some time in restoring order.

During their absence the reinforcements drawn by Villars from his centre had brought the Allies to a standstill. The return of Eugene put fresh life into them, and, as Withers increased his pressure upon their flank, the French gave way. Gradually they were thrust back through the forest to the plateau beyond, where they began to re-form, while their pursuers sorted themselves out as best they could along the edge of the forest. Villars thus in time arrayed some fifty battalions on the plateau, and was about to lead them to a counter-attack when he was struck by a musket-ball below the knee. Unable to keep his seat in his saddle, he called for a chair, but fainting from pain, was carried off

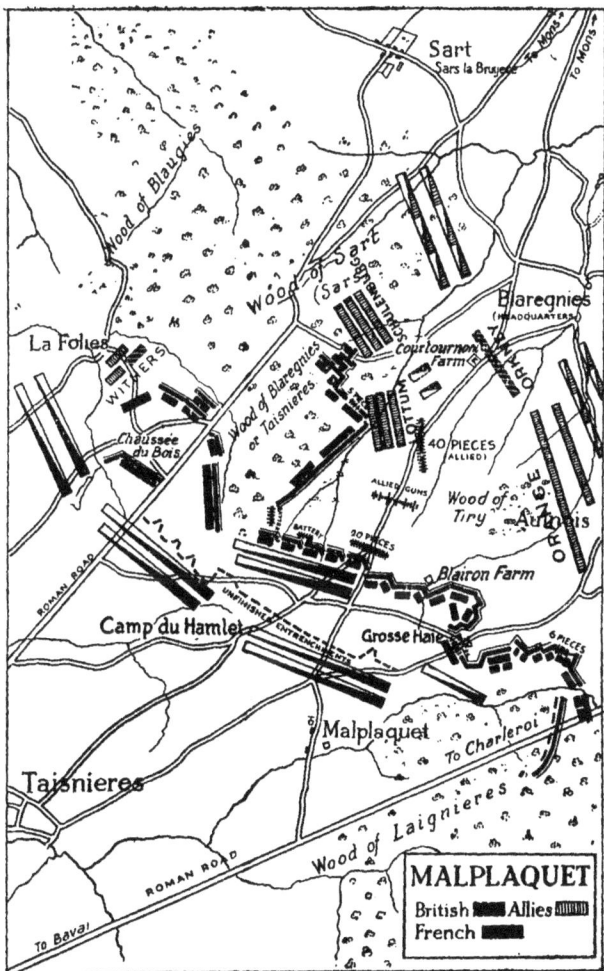

Sart
Sars la Bruyère
To Mons
To Mons

Wood of Blaugies

Wood of Sart
(Sars)

Blaregnies
(HEADQUARTERS)

La Folies

WITHERS

Courtournon
Farm

Chaussée
du Bois

Wood of Blaregnies
or Taisnieres

ORKNEY

40 PIECES
(ALLIED)

ALLIED GUNS

Wood of
Tiry

Artois

BATTERY

30 PIECES

Blairon Farm

ROMAN ROAD

Camp du Hamlet

UNFINISHED ENTRENCHMENTS

Grosse Haie

6 PIECES

Malplaquet

To Charleroi

Taisnieres

ROMAN ROAD

Wood of Laignieres

To Baval

MALPLAQUET

British   Allies
French

the field. No one seems to have taken his place, and Eugene, himself wounded in the head, re-formed his infantry on the western fringe of the wood, and, bringing up seven guns, compelled the French cavalry to fall back out of range.

Then Marlborough, seeing that the moment was come for the true attack on the centre, launched Orkney's British battalions at the entrenchments and carried them at the first rush. The British remained in them lining the parados while Marlborough brought forward guns upon either flank to sweep the ground beyond. Then the first line of the Allied cavalry advanced, and was forming on the other side of the entrenchments when it was borne back by a vigorous charge of the French horse. But these in turn were repulsed by the fire of the British infantry. And then ensued a succession of combats of cavalry which swayed backward and forward with varying fortune until Eugene threw in the last reserves. During this time other squadrons fell upon the flank of the French right while the Allied Dutch infantry assailed it in front ; and the French right wing likewise was forced back. But the French cavalry, though worsted at the last, had gained time for the main body to make an orderly retreat ; and so after six hours of desperate fighting the battle of Malplaquet came to an end.

The casualties of the French numbered about eleven thousand, but those of the Allies were twice as great. The presumption and conceit of the Prince of Orange had deranged all the plans of Marlborough and Eugene, and the mischief that he wrought was not bounded by the battle. The Dutch were dismayed, as well they might be, by the useless slaughter of their best men, and the French were correspondingly heartened. Marlborough and Eugene had hoped to make an end of their enemy and of the war, and they had failed. No two other men would, in the circumstances, have averted defeat; and they reaped at least some harvest of victory by the capture of Mons, which served the useful purpose of covering their conquests in Flanders and Brabant. But what was needed was a second Ramillies, and for this Malplaquet, even with the acquisition of Tournai and Mons, was but a sorry substitute.

XV

THROUGHOUT the campaign Marlborough had
been plagued to intervene in party squabbles,
which he abominated, and on his return home
he found his position sensibly weakened. The
breach between the Duchess and the Queen
was widened ; the influence of the rival favourite, Mrs. Masham, was increased ; and Robert
Harley was using her for steady undermining of
the Government which had so far conducted the
war with France. Marlborough now made the
bad blunder of asking to be appointed Commander-in-Chief for his life. The request, being
tactless and unprecedented, was rightly refused by Anne ; and Marlborough, shaken out
of his usual serenity by worry, fatigue, and
trouble with his eyesight, received the rebuff
with culpably ill grace. Then Anne made a bad
mistake. She filled up the vacant Colonelcy of
a regiment by the appointment of Colonel Hill,
on the nomination of his sister Mrs. Masham,
ignoring the Commander-in-Chief. Marlborough naturally decided to resign at once

and to insist that either he or Mrs. Masham must go ; but after much hesitation he was persuaded to consent to a compromise, which Anne regarded as a victory for herself. It was difficult for a really patriotic man, such as Marlborough, to judge how best he could serve his country amid such a maze of intrigue.

His enemies none the less were anxious to get him out of England ; and this they effected, at Harley's instance, by sending him to take part in the negotiations, over which he had not the slightest control, with France at the Hague. The atmosphere of hostility was ever present with him : ' I have never in this war,' he wrote, ' gone into the field with so heavy a heart as at this time.' And again: 'If I considered myself, I would not serve one minute longer.' However, he began operations with Eugene in April by a skilful manœuvre which carried his army across the lines of La Bassée, and then laid siege to Douai. The matter sounds simple when set down in a few words, and Marlborough himself made little of it except to remark, on 22nd April, that ' the poor soldiers ' had had no rest. For in all these operations Marlborough compassed his ends by swift and skilful movements which of themselves would have brought fame to any other general. Villars talked loudly of relieving Douai, but Marlborough felt rightly confident that the Marshal would not risk a battle. Douai fell on the 26th of June, and Marlborough contemplated next the siege of Arras on the innermost line of the French frontier-defences. But Villars' dispositions forbade this enterprise ; and moreover he had constructed a new and unassailable series of entrenchments which he declared would be Marlborough's *ne plus ultra*. The Duke therefore turned to the sieges in succession of Béthune, Aire and St. Venant, all of which fortresses made a spirited resistance, their capture costing some fifteen thousand casualties. Much though he hated sieges he was acting with extreme caution, knowing that the slightest failure would mean not only his own fall, but the ascendency of unscrupulous politicians who would not hesitate to sacrifice all the triumphs of the war to factious ends.

Aire did not surrender until the 13th of November ; but long before then the worst had happened at home. The Government had fallen. Godolphin had been dismissed, and Harley had been appointed Lord-Treasurer in his place. The Duke returned to England on the 26th of December, and very shortly afterwards the Duchess was dismissed from all of her appointments. Apart from this great blow there was no end to petty persecution. Adam Cardonnel was removed from his place as Secretary at War—Military Secretary would be a correcter interpretation of his functions in those days—without the slightest reference to the Duke. The Queen required Marlborough to forbid the moving of any vote of thanks to him in Parliament. Three generals who had drunk Marlborough's health with confusion to his enemies were turned out of the Army. There were even a few officers who, to the disgust and contempt of their fellows, turned against him. The mouths of every libeller and slanderer were opened ; and two of them, St. John and Swift, were mighty with tongue and pen. Nothing was too base to be insinuated against the Duke. Marlborough, they said, was prolonging the war for his own ends ; he could make peace but he would not ; he delighted in bloodshed ; and, as a climax, he had neither personal courage nor military talent. Such is the vileness and meanness of mankind. ' I suppose,' wrote Marlborough bitterly, ' that I must every summer venture my life in battle, and be found fault with in the winter for not bringing home peace, though I wish for it with all my heart and soul.'

His natural desire was to resign ; but he was
overborne by the remonstrances of Godolphin
and Eugene, who entreated him to hold the
Grand Alliance together for yet a little longer
so as to gain for Europe an honourable peace.
They were unaware that Harley and his gang
were already secretly opening negotiations with
Louis xiv. which were to dissolve the Alliance
and yield to France practically all that Europe
had fought for ten years to withhold from her.
These men, who accused Marlborough of wilful
squandering of human lives, scrupled not to
send brave soldiers to their death for a cause
which they had made up their minds to betray.
Probably they hoped that some lucky shot might
rid them of Marlborough himself. In any case,
the Duke went out to his last campaign en-
compassed by secret enemies and spies, watching eagerly for any false step, for any act that
might give an opening for slander or accusation. Everything by chance conspired against
Marlborough. The Emperor Joseph died of
smallpox, which signified the almost certain
succession of the Archduke Charles to the Imperial crown, and the renunciation of his claim
to the Spanish throne. A breach in the Grand
Alliance might very probably follow ; but—a
still greater blow to Marlborough — Prince

Eugene would almost certainly be kept away from Flanders. Marlborough's force had already been weakened by the need for supplying garrisons to the towns captured in 1710 ; and the English Government deliberately weakened it still further by taking from him five battalions which were sent on a useless expedition to Newfoundland under command of Mrs. Masham's brainless brother, Colonel Hill. Meanwhile Villars lay behind his lines—his boasted *ne plus ultra*—which ran eastward along the course of the Canche from its mouth at Montreuil to Arras, and on by Bouchain to Valenciennes. Their total length was of some eighty-five miles, the greater part of the distance secured by swamp and inundation and the remainder by earthworks. Villars had strict orders not to fight, for Louis was well aware of the course of politics in England, and hoped to gain his point without a blow. So, a century later, Masséna lingered at incredible sacrifice before the lines of Torres Vedras, hoping that faction in England would ensure for him the withdrawal of Wellington's army from the Peninsula. England's enemies can always count upon at least some help from Westminster.

XVI

MARLBOROUGH took the field in May, the Imperial army being still with him, though without Eugene. Villars lay with his right at Bouchain, his line extending from thence about ten miles westward. Marlborough took post opposite to him, and both forces remained inactive for six weeks, until Eugene arrived, and on departing took the Imperial troops away with him. To conceal this diminution of his army Marlborough moved one march westward to the plain of Lens, where he offered battle. He had now only ninety-four battalions and one hundred and forty-five squadrons against one hundred and thirty-one battalions and one hundred and eighty-seven squadrons of the French ; but Villars simply moved opposite to him behind his impregnable lines, obeying his orders not to hazard a fight.

Nevertheless Marlborough was determined to pass these lines somehow, and had thought out his plans. The inundation of the River

Sensée could be traversed only by two cause-
ways, the one at Arleux, half-way between
Arras and Bouchain, and the other at Aubigny,
five miles to east of Arleux. The post at Arleux
was defended by a strong fort. Marlborough
knew that he could take this fort at any time,
but that Villars would certainly retake and re-
build it as soon as his back was turned. He
therefore set himself to beguile Villars into de-
molishing it himself; and he went to work
thus. He sent a strong detachment to capture
the fort, which was done without difficulty,
and then gave orders for the works to be
greatly strengthened, also posting a large
force under the Prussian General Hompesch
at Douai, about three miles to north of it, for
its further protection. Chance played into his
hands. Hompesch, thinking the fort secure
so near the guns of Douai, neglected the most
elementary precautions and was surprised only
two days later by a sudden attack from Villars
upon Arleux. The French were only repulsed
with difficulty and not without shame to the
defenders, and Villars was in ecstasies over his
success. Marlborough, for the benefit of the
spies that surrounded him, manifested considerable annoyance, reinforced the garrison
of Arleux, and pushed forward its new defence

with energy, to show the importance that he attached to it. When all was completed he threw a weak detachment into the fort, and moved the main army two miles to westward. Villars followed him on a parallel course, but did not forget before he started to send a sufficient body of troops to attack Arleux. The commandant of the garrison promptly informed Marlborough that he was too weak to hold the fort, and Marlborough at once despatched Cadogan with a strong force to relieve it. It was noticed that Cadogan, however, did not hurry himself, and before he had marched half-way to the place he returned with the news that Arleux had surrendered.

Villars was immensely elated, and Marlborough for the first time in his life seemed to be greatly upset. Throwing off his wonted calm, he publicly declared with passion that he would yet be even with Villars, and would attack him where he lay at whatever cost. Then came the news that Villars had razed all the works at Arleux to the ground ; and Marlborough, recalling all the pains that he had spent upon it, evinced worse temper than ever. He vowed that he would avenge this insult to his army, and reiterated his menace of a direct attack upon Villars's entrenchments. Villars,

fully apprised of this outburst, detached a force
to make a diversion in Brabant; and this
movement seemed to drive Marlborough to
distraction. Swearing that he would check
the march of this detachment, he sent ten
thousand men to Béthune, nearly twenty miles
north of Arras, and the whole of his baggage
and heavy artillery to Douai. Having thus
weakened an army which was already numeri-
cally inferior to the French, he repaired the
roads that led towards the enemy's entrenchments and with much display of wrath,
vindictiveness and general ill-temper advanced the main body a march nearer to
Villars's lines. His army watched him with
amazement, for they had never looked for
such behaviour from their loved and trusted
Corporal John.

Villars, meanwhile, was delighted beyond
measure. He drew every man from all parts
of his lines and from the neighbouring garrisons
to the threatened point, and asked for nothing
better than that Marlborough should attack.
The Duke maintained his strange demeanour,
and seemed inseparably wedded to his mad
design. On the 2nd of August he advanced
to within a league of the lines, and set the
whole of his cavalry to make fascines, prepara-

tory to an assault. At nightfall of the 3rd he sent away under cover of darkness the whole of his field artillery and every scrap of the remaining baggage, and on the 4th he rode out, attended by all his generals and eighty squadrons of cavalry, to reconnoitre the lines in full view of the enemy. He had now resumed his wonted serenity, and spoke with every confidence of success, pointing out to each subordinate commander the place and the manner of the attack. The generals listened, but could not help seeing that the entire plan was madness. In the middle of the proceedings Cadogan turned his horse, unnoticed, and galloped back to camp at the top of his speed. The Duke presently turned also, and riding back very slowly to his quarters issued detailed orders for an attack on the morrow.

Therewith all ranks of the army, from highest to lowest, sank into unfathomable depression. How could an assault succeed when a great part of the army and the whole of the artillery had been detached to other service ? The most part gave themselves up for lost, and lamented loudly that the Old Corporal must have lost his wits ; and beyond doubt the tidings of this despairing spirit soon found its way to Villars.

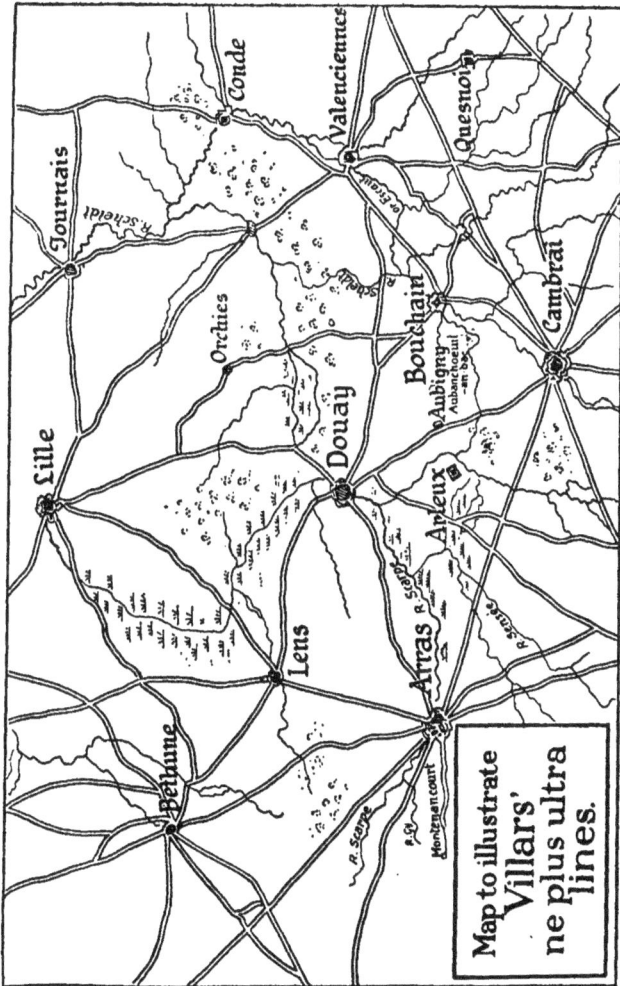

Map to illustrate
Villars'
ne plus ultra
lines.

K

Only a very small remnant ventured to hope that Corporal John might still have some surprise in store for them ; but the afternoon of that 4th of August was one of dismal despondency in Marlborough's camp.

But meanwhile Cadogan with an escort of forty hussars had been galloping hard over the plain of Lens to Douai, fifteen miles away. There he found Hompesch, now strengthened by detachments from Béthune and elsewhere to a strength of twelve thousand foot and two thousand horse, all ready for him, and told him that the time was come. Hompesch thereupon issued orders for his troops to march that night. Still the main army of Marlborough, knowing nothing of this, remained gloomy and apprehensive until the sun went down and the drummers came forward to beat tattoo. Then a column of the Allied cavalry trotted out and turned to westward in full view of the French army, stirring every French brain with curiosity as to the meaning of the movement. Then the drums began to roll ; darkness fell, and the order was quietly passed down the line to strike tents and prepare to march immediately.

Despondency passed away and confidence returned. Corporal John had not failed his men after all. In an hour all was ready, and four columns of march were formed. The cavalry, having fulfilled their mission of distracting French attention to the wrong quarter, returned under cover of night to the camp. At nine o'clock the whole army faced to eastward and marched off in silence, with Marlborough himself at the head of the vanguard. The night was fine and Marlborough had carefully studied the hour of moonrise, so that the columns had moonlight to help them. Then the moon paled before the first flush of dawn, and the columns reached the River Scarpe, having so far covered fifteen miles in eight hours. On the farther bank stood the field artillery, punctual to time, and pontoon bridges were laid for the army to cross. Then a messenger came to Marlborough with a note saying that General Hompesch had passed the causeway at Arleux at 3 a.m. and was in possession of the enemy's lines. The Duke at once trotted forward with fifty squadrons of horse. The remainder of the cavalry halted to form a rearguard, and the infantry, hearing the good news, stepped out with a will to forward the plans of Corporal John.

Villars was apprised of Marlborough's march no more than two hours after its beginning, but

he was so thoroughly puzzled by the Duke's
wiles that he did not fathom their true intent
until three hours later. Then, frantic with
vexation, he put himself at the head of the
Household Cavalry and galloped off to eastward. So furiously rode he that he tired out all
but about one hundred troopers, and pressed
on with these alone. But even so he was too
late. Marlborough, using the causeway next
below that of Arleux, had passed a strong body
of cavalry over the Scarpe to bar all advance
from the west, and Villars blundering into the
midst of these lost the whole of his escort and
narrowly escaped capture himself. Riding
back, he waited impatiently for the arrival of
his own main body of horse ; but the Allied
infantry had caught sight of it on the march and
was racing it with ardour for the causeway at
Arleux. Hundreds of the tramping foot-soldiers
dropped down unconscious from fatigue and
not a few died where they lay, but the survivors
pushed on without a halt and came quickly
into their positions. The right wing of infantry
crossed the Scarpe at 4 p.m., having traversed
close upon forty miles in eighteen hours. By
5 p.m. all the troops that had come in were
drawn up south of the river within striking distance of Arras, Cambrai and Bouchain.

For the next three days stragglers kept pouring in, and Marlborough made no movement, though Villars ventured to march forward and offer him battle under the walls of Cambrai. The Dutch deputies, who had prevented the Duke so often from fighting when he wished, now pressed him urgently to action when he did not wish : a perverse and treacherous tribe. Marlborough's own design was to beleaguer Bouchain ; and now the deputies shrank from the danger of a siege carried on by an inferior under the eyes of a superior force. Marlborough put the paltry creatures aside and went his own way. On the 7th of August he passed the whole of his troops across the Scheldt unhindered by Villars, and covered the siege-works so skilfully that the Marshal was powerless to effect the relief of the place. The Dutch deputies, as usual, intervened at one critical moment to entreat the Duke to raise the siege, but he was inexorable, and Bouchain surrendered under the very eyes of Villars on the 2nd of September. Marlborough would have followed up this success with the siege of Quesnoi, and Harley wrote him many specious letters to encourage him in the project, though by this time the minister had come to an agreement with Louis XIV. that

149

England should forsake the Grand Alliance. Harley took care, therefore, that the operations should proceed no further, and with the capture of Bouchain Marlborough's military career came to an end.

XVII

MARLBOROUGH came home in November to find
himself at the mercy of his unscrupulous enemies.
The House of Commons in the preceding May
had ordered an enquiry into abuses in the public
expenditure ; and the Duke was charged with
fraud, extortion and embezzlement. The pre-
text for this accusation was that he had received
the commission, already mentioned, upon the
contract from the bread-contractors, for the
expense of obtaining intelligence ; the sum
total amounting in all to over £63,000. Marlborough proved conclusively that this perqui-
site was regularly allowed to the Commander-
in-Chief in Flanders, for that particular purpose.
He even added the voluntary admission that
he had deducted two and a half per cent. from
the pay of foreign troops, with the same object.
This defence was absolutely valid and sound ;
but no defence would have been accepted by
the faction that then ruled England, and on the
31st of December he was dismissed from all
public employment.

Three weeks later the House of Commons

voted that the acceptance of the perquisites mentioned above was unwarrantable and illegal, and directed that Marlborough should be prosecuted by the Attorney-General. The Ministry then appointed the Duke of Ormonde to be Commander-in-Chief in Marlborough's place, and confirmed to him those same unwarrantable and illegal perquisites. The faction was affected by no sense of logic, much less by any sense of shame.

The long intrigues with France issued finally in the Peace of Utrecht in April 1713, whereby was sacrificed practically every object for which the war had been fought. Insult and persecution of Marlborough had meanwhile continued, and had been extended to his principal officers, such as Cadogan. In November 1712 the Duke left England, a self-banished man, and repaired as a disgraced Englishman to the Low Countries. There all ranks and conditions spontaneously united to do him honour. At Ostend, at Antwerp, at Maastricht the garrisons were under arms to receive him, the guns thundered out a salute, and the population welcomed him with joyful acclamations. He made his way to Aix-la-Chapelle, where the Duchess presently joined him, and from thence to Frankfurt, always comforted by the confidence and sympathy of Eugene. Incidentally, under the treaty of Utrecht his principality of Mindelheim was taken from him and restored to the Elector of Bavaria, nor, apart from the empty title, did he ever receive any indemnity in lieu, despite of Eugene's utmost efforts on his behalf. From Frankfurt he finally removed to Antwerp, whence he anxiously watched the course of political affairs in England.

He did not wait long. In July 1714, Harley, now Earl of Oxford, having quarrelled with St. John, was dismissed from office ; and St. John formed a Jacobite administration. Queen Anne, however, was at the moment sick unto death, and the Whig leaders quietly ousted St. John and assured the succession of the House of Hanover. Eighteen Lords Justices were appointed by the new King to carry on the Government pending his arrival from Hanover, but Marlborough's name was not included among them. He crossed over to England on the day after the Queen's death, and was enthusiastically received both when he landed and when he reached London. He was reinstated in his old places of Commander-in-Chief, now a purely honorary office, and of Master-General of the Ordnance, but was admitted to no share in the Government beyond his departmental duties. He had some little part, as Commander-in-Chief, in the suppression of the rebellion of 1715, though he delegated the active work in the field to Cadogan. In 1716 he suffered two successive attacks of paralysis, in May and in November, which impaired his speech, though not his intellect, for he continued to attend to his duties in the House of Lords almost to the end. He resigned his appointments, and though the King refused to accept his resignation, the Duke thenceforward counted for little even in his own departments. His work was in fact done, and the period of rest was at hand. He made his last appearance in the House of Lords on the 27th of November 1721. In June 1722 he was smitten by a third attack of paralysis, and, after lying perfectly conscious for some days, died at dawn of the 16th of June 1722. Three weeks later, on the 6th of July, he was buried with gorgeous ceremonial in Westminster Abbey ; and at his funeral there were used for the first time the commands which are now heard at the burial of the humblest British soldier : ' Reverse Arms,' ' Rest on your arms reversed.' From the Abbey the body was shortly afterwards removed to Blenheim, where it now rests.

XVIII

MARLBOROUGH presents one of the rarest of the combinations to be found in the human creature, that of personal charm and fascination united with genius. Napoleon certainly possessed genius, and, apart from all other records, I chance to know by oral tradition from one who had conversed with him that his manner and smile were irresistible. But Napoleon could be vulgar and violent and foul-mouthed ; he could and did sometimes behave, to speak plainly, like a little cad. There was nothing of this about Marlborough. Delicate, sensitive, and fastidious, he abhorred anything that savoured of the coarse, the intemperate or the licentious. Imperturbably sweet-tempered and gentle, he diffused about him an atmosphere of moderation and calm, which heightened the natural influence of his personality. I cannot conceive that Marlborough can have entered, however quietly, any room, however crowded, but that he made his presence immediately and imperceptibly felt. We know that physically he

155

was very attractive, and though we are told
nothing of his voice, I cannot believe but that
it must have been peculiarly winning. His
address was modest and deferential, and his
courtesy spontaneous and unaffected. In fact
his natural instinct was to please—to please
every one, high or low. That he bore himself
with the dignity that comes of self-respect is no
more than we should look for from such a man,
but no one could conceive of Marlborough as
pompous, or self-important. He was far too
great a man for that.

And behind all these outward graces there
was the transcendent insight which saw men
and things not as other men see them but as
they are. He cannot have been very highly
educated, as scholars understand the word. It
has been said that he knew no more of English
history than is to be learned from Shakespeare's
plays. But he had graduated early in the study
of human nature, and he must have been quick
of apprehension and tenacious of memory;
otherwise he could never have mastered the
briefs that were given to him for his diplomatic
missions, whether as mediator between Charles
II. and his brother James, or between the Court
of St. James's and the Courts of Europe. But
towards such work, as towards all other, tran-

scendent common sense was of incomparable help, since it taught him to ignore all matters but the essential. Rarely do we find in one man so discerning a grasp alike of the essential great and the essential little things of life.

He used his great endowments first to raise himself in life. He was conscious of them, and was ambitious of power. But his beginnings were humble, one might almost call them menial, and he had to walk warily, for he lived in troubled times and the ways were slippery. Thus he became early a past master in the art of dissimulation ; and if this mastery were turned to mean account when he retained the confidence of James up to the very eve of his desertion, it was employed wholly in the service of his country when he deceived all the spies and enemies round about him, all the commanders of the opposing armies, and even all of his own officers and men in that marvellous campaign of 1711. Quite early, too, he became very careful of money, as a poor man must be, and he retained that carefulness because wealth is a means to power. There was much talk of his avarice among his detractors, political and other, most probably because he was observed to be specially parcimonious in the matter of

157

petty expenses. But I have noticed that men who, starting with nothing, have attained great wealth, will give away thousands without a murmur, but will bitterly resent paying six-pence for goods which they value—and rightly value—at threepence. They demand their money's worth, and from long self-training will not countenance waste. Marlborough died immensely rich ; but let it be remembered that he refused in succession a large pension when he obtained his dukedom, the Governorship of the Netherlands, which he ardently coveted for the position quite apart from its huge emolu-ments, and that he rejected a gigantic bribe from the Court of France to grant that country favourable terms of peace.

His greatness in war has obscured his extreme skill as a diplomatist. And first account must be taken of the physical strain which must have been imposed by long journeys in the autumn and winter after all the anxieties and fatigues of active service in the field. A man between fifty and sixty was far older two hundred years ago than one of the same age in the twentieth century. Travelling, unless it were by boat on canal or river, was uncomfortable and exhaust-ing. Bad roads made long journeys, whether in coach or in the saddle, both tedious and

trying. Bad weather might cause the delay
of days in some cheerless and comfortless halt-
ing-place. Yet after such travel it was expected that a man should have full command
of his temper, ready courtesy and infinite
patience. He must submit to have his time
wasted by pompous ceremonies for the exalta-
tion of small potentates, and by wearisome
circumlocution of nervous ministers. He had
to bear himself at once with the dignity of
Queen Anne's representative, with the friendly
deference of a colleague and an ally, and with
the unobtrusive ascendency of the supreme
guide and counsellor. Above all he had to
bear in mind the vagaries of Parliament and
the incessant intrigues of faction at home. Yet
from mission after mission Marlborough returned with success, and apparently effortless
success ; and the fact was accepted as a matter
of course. Nations have often pinned their
faith to one man to redeem them out of all
their troubles ; but hardly one such man could
show as few failures as Marlborough. There
have been charming men, there have been long-
suffering men, there have been wise men, yet
few have, like Marlborough, combined charm,
patience and wisdom.

But after all it is as a soldier that Marlborough

chiefly lives in human memory, and people are inclined to regard him as a soldier only. Yet the very greatest soldiers have always been also great civil administrators, while Caesar was further a great literary artist. The use of technical terms blinds ordinary folk to the fact that the rules of strategy and tactics are after all dictated by common sense, and that the business of war is but one branch of the general government of men. In theory war supersedes all civil law, and a commander-in-chief is vested with absolute powers. But civil autocrats have claimed the like authority in time of peace, and have exercised it as fully as any general. The truth is that civil communities, even as armies, must be led, not driven, if they are to make the best of themselves, and Marlborough was above all things a leader.

Let us take first what may be called his material work for the Army. He supplied the infantry with a new and improved musket, and drew up for it a new and simplified method of drill. He was very exacting as to fire discipline, and would put the whole army through its platoon exercises by signal of flag and drum before his own eye. The cavalry he taught to employ shock action instead of missile action —futile firing from the saddle—and in 1707 he issued to the horse the breast-piece of a cuirass, which gave them protection only for so long as they did not turn their backs. To the artillery he devoted particular attention, with the result that by superhuman exertions the gunners managed to draw all their guns from the Rhine to the Danube.

Next, let us turn to the moral work. Marlborough was most careful always that his men should be well fed and regularly paid ; and, though he enforced the strictest discipline, he was not only their commander but their friend. He felt deeply for their sufferings and hardships, and, as we have seen from a letter to his wife, their cheers and their welcome to him in the field almost unmanned him. There were plenty of ruffians in the ranks, but his own gentleness, fastidiousness and abhorrence of loose conduct or coarse language filtered down to them ; and Marlborough's soldiers had above all things self-respect. Their devotion to him is shown by the extraordinary efforts which they made to execute his manœuvres, no matter how long and fatiguing the marches. Their confidence in him is proved by the willingness with which they obeyed him even when he deceived them into thinking that he had lost his wits. Never was commander more dearly

L   161

loved, nor more enthusiastically followed, than Corporal John.

With the officers, or at any rate with some of them, he had more difficulty, because they could use political influence to bear upon the Secretary at War who, when Marlborough was absent from England,enjoyed enormous powers. The peculiar system which then prevailed, whereby officers bought their commissions, owned their companies and battalions, and provided their own recruits and remounts, frequently imposed upon them great hardship, which could only be relieved by the help of the State. But the hostility of the English nation to a standing army was so virulent and deeply rooted that it was dangerous to call upon the State to make good the losses of officers. It would, indeed, probably have repudiated any obligations of the kind directly that peace had been concluded. Marlborough, therefore, braved all unpopularity that he might incur with his officers by holding the balance as justly as he could between them and their employers. He did intercede to secure the State's assistance for the widows of officers who died on service, for therein he held that the officers had a real grievance. But it never occurred to him to court favour with his officers by becoming their

champion against their ill-treatment by Parliament, which many a smaller man and less
honourable public servant might have felt
tempted to do. In the field, of course, he commanded the loyal devotion and confidence of
officers not less than of men. He had an eye
for the smallest detail. An officer has re-
corded how he was left with his company
isolated in a dangerously advanced position,
and how the Duke himself, 'always watch-
ful, always right,' recalled him before it was
too late. Such trifling incidents help us to
realise that, while Corporal John was with
them, every officer and man felt that all was
well.

As to the work of Marlborough's staff it is
extremely difficult to speak. Cadogan, who
was its chief, was undoubtedly a man of remarkable energy and ability, with, moreover, a
happy knack of making all wheels run smoothly;
but staff officers who knew their business were
very rare in those days, and the few that existed
must have been much overworked. There is a
small collection of papers at Windsor Castle
that belonged to one of Cadogan's assistants—a
certain Captain King—from which it appears
that at the siege of Menin this same King acted
at one and the same moment as a captain of

infantry, commanding engineer, commanding artillery officer, assistant quartermaster-general, and ordnance store-officer. King once incurred Marlborough's censure. Adam Cardonnel wrote to him that ' my lord duke is surprised,' and King evidently took care not to awake my lord duke's surprise again, for he presently won Marlborough's praise. ' His Grace sees your zeal and diligence,' wrote Cardonnel, ' and I dare say will have so just a sense of it as to do justice to your merit upon the first occasion that offers.' Such was the tone of the correspondence on Marlborough's staff, reflecting always the courtesy and serenity of the great chief.

The management of all the foreign units of Marlborough's army must have been intensely difficult, looking to all the pretensions and jealousies or royal highnesses, serene highnesses, and all the hierarchy of the *Almanach de Gotha.* Yet Marlborough had the happy gift of making them work together as could no other man. This must have cost an infinity of little compliments, little attentions, little thoughtfulnesses, which no doubt took up much time and interrupted work that seemed more important. But much of Marlborough's strength lay in his estimation of the importance of such matters and on the distinction which he unconsciously drew between a driver and a leader.

As to his actual work in the field, we have often only the wreck of his finest conceptions, ruined as they were by the jealousy, selfishness, timidity and conceit of smaller men. His favourite plan to invade France by the line of the Moselle, for instance, never came to maturity at all, and he was condemned to fritter away his energies, much against his will, among the maze of fortresses on the French northern frontier. But in every campaign we find the same characteristics. He seems to take the measure of his adversaries exactly. He bewilders them thoroughly by movements which all lead up to his own design, and then suddenly he appears at the decisive point before he is expected, and strikes hard before his enemies have well realised that he is in their presence at all. He snatches not only the initiative but the ascendency, and forces his adversaries to bow to it. They can never divine what he will do next, for he scorns all pedantic rules and is a law unto himself. Yet for all that, he is no gambler but a cool calculator. He takes liberties with his foes, but shows no overweening carelessness. It could not be said of him, as Lord Wellesley said of Napoleon, that his was a nature that prepared for itself great reverses ; and that was perhaps one reason why he never fought a battle which he did not win nor besieged a fortress which he did not take. He was sober-minded, and he was deeply religious. He believed in and feared the Lord of Hosts, and knew his own littleness in the sight of God.

Lastly, amid all his triumphs, whether in the Court or in the field, there is one thing greater than fame, greater even than the exultant cheers of the men who would have gone through hell with him, and that is to bear himself worthily of the wife whom he loves. She stands first with him at all times, and repeated letters must assure her of the fact. Scores of women during his campaigns and his diplomatic missions must have tried to steal a man so comely, so fascinating and so eminent, but they tried in vain. Sarah remains the only woman in the world to him. He was the ideal husband, always thoughtful, never ill-tempered, always understanding, and a lover from the first day of his courtship to the last day of his life.

Sarah of course had her faults, so many and so glaring that the unthinking are apt to sneer at Marlborough's unchanging devotion to her and to hint, to use a vulgar expression, that he was hen-pecked. Sarah was doubtless self-willed, ambitious and clever, a violent partisan and an admirable hater. But, when all is said and done, Sarah lives in history solely in virtue of the reflected glory of her great husband. There are plenty of clever women, but there is a great gulf fixed between a clever woman and a wise man. That she became intolerably unreasonable and latterly almost impossible is easily accounted for by a simple physical cause. She was forty-two years of age when she received the shattering blow of her son's death. She was forty-seven when she began to quarrel seriously with the Queen. We see parallel cases every day of women who at this age become difficult, at any rate for a time, and sometimes remain so until the day of their death. Marlborough, doubtless fully aware of the true state of affairs, was more than ever loyal, gentle and indulgent to her, as was his duty to the woman that he loved. No doubt Sarah was trying in still earlier days. The story of her cutting off her beautiful hair to mortify her adoring husband must belong to a time when it had not turned grey. But that she was ever otherwise than proud of her husband and devoted to him, and that he was not

167

master in all essential things, I do not believe. After his death the mother of one of the Sheffields, Dukes of Buckingham (the former owners of Buckingham Palace), wrote to Sarah to borrow Marlborough's funeral car for the interment of her son. Sarah answered very curtly that the car had carried the body of My Lord of Marlborough, and should certainly carry no other. And there spoke the real woman.

It is this touching simplicity of his wedded love which makes Marlborough so human to us, despite of his gigantic stature. For a giant he was, not only among Englishmen but among the great men of the world, not merely a genius but a perfectly sane genius, ' the greatest statesman,' in the words of an erratic genius, Henry St. John, ' and the greatest general that this country or any other country has produced.' There is no statue of him in London, and he needs none. If there had been no Marlborough England would have sunk into a mere province of France, and the United States would have been French, not English. There would have been no occasion for our first port, which Marlborough gave us, in the Mediterranean. There would have been no England as we know it, and no British Empire. Centuries hence, when historians write their account of an England which has become a mere name and of an Europe which has passed away, they will be silent about many men who are now reckoned great, but they will not pass over Marlborough.

BIBLIOGRAPHICAL NOTE

THE standard Life of Marlborough is still the dull
biography of Coxe, eked out by that of Lediard.
Mr. Frank Taylor's new Life, if completed, would
and should have superseded them, but it was
unfortunately cut short by the writer's death.
There is some merit in a French biography in
three volumes, which was written by Napoleon's
order. Lord Wolseley's work is a not very valuable
fragment. The five volumes of Marlborough's
despatches are indispensable. There are useful
details in the autobiography of Captain Parker,
and in the diaries of Serjeant Millner and Deane,
and of General Stearne, the last named being known
to me only through extracts in Cannon's history of
the 18th Royal Irish. There is very valuable in-
formation in the *Orkney Papers*, published by the
Historical MSS. Commission. The French printed
sources are very freely given in Mr. Frank Taylor's
work, but I may mention specially the Memoirs
of Saint-Simon and of Villars. I found little in
the Public Record Office beyond the Secretary's
Common Letter Books, which are useful for the
general history of the army under Queen Anne.
The French archives for this period I fear that I
have not studied.

INDEX

171

173

INDEX

Tallard, 34, 42, 44, 47, 48, 50, 54, 56, 62, 64, 65, 68, 70, 71, 73, 74, 75

Tangier, 7

Turenne, 7

Utrecht, Peace of, 152

Vauban, 118

Vendôme, 104, 107, 110, 111, 112, 115, 116, 117, 118, 119, 120

Villars, Marshal, 31, 42, 43, 44, 92, 104, 107, 124, 126, 127, 129, 130, 135, 136, 139, 140, 141, 142, 143, 144, 147, 148, 149

Villeroi, 47, 48, 54, 56, 78, 82, 85, 87, 88, 89, 93, 94, 96, 99, 100, 101, 104

Webb, General, 120

Wellesley, Lord, 165

Wellington, Duke of, 51, 139

William III. (as Prince of Orange), 9, 13, 14 ; King of England, 15, 16, 17, 18, 19, 20, 22, 23, 25, 41

Withers, 129, 130

York, Duchess of, 6, 9 ; household of, 8

York, Duke of, 7, 9, 10, 12 ; household of, 8